THE NOLAN RYAN BEEF & BARBECUE COOKBOOK

THE
NOLAN RYAN
BEEF & BARBECUE COOKBOOK

RECIPES FROM A TEXAS KITCHEN

NOLAN RYAN

WITH JR ROSENTHAL   PHOTOGRAPHY BY GENO LORO

LB

LITTLE, BROWN AND COMPANY
NEW YORK   BOSTON   LONDON

Little, Brown and Company
Hachette Book Group
237 Park Avenue, New York, NY 10017
littlebrown.com

First Edition: May 2014

Little, Brown and Company is a division of Hachette Book Group, Inc. The
Little, Brown name and logo are trademarks of Hachette Book Group, Inc.

The publisher is not responsible for websites (or their content) that are
not owned by the publisher.

The Hachette Speakers Bureau provides a wide range of authors for
speaking events. To find out more, go to hachettespeakersbureau.com or
call (866) 376-6591.

Photography credits: pp. viii and 4–5 copyright Ernie Gill; p. 2 copyright
Kelly Gavin; pp. 9, 11, and all recipe photographs copyright Geno Loro.

Food styling by Angela Yeung and Jennie Kelley

ISBN 978-0-316-24826-6
LCCN 2013956724

10 9 8 7 6 5 4 3 2 1

Printed in China

FOR MY MOTHER,
Martha Lee Ryan

CONTENTS

THE EDUCATION OF A CATTLEMAN

BY NOLAN RYAN, WITH RUTH, WENDY, REESE & REID RYAN

On a warm and windy day in April in my hometown of Alvin, Texas, a very special place for my family and me, I announced to my parents—at the age of ten—that I was ready to get into the cattle business.

I talked my parents into taking me to visit a dairy farmer who was a member of our church, and I bought a day-old calf from him and started bottle-feeding it. I went back the next week to buy another calf, and that was the first time I learned about price increases, because the first calf cost a dollar fifty and the second (only ten days later) cost two dollars.

I built up my small herd to about seven heifers, but once I got into junior high school and started playing football, basketball, and baseball, I decided to sell the heifers. That was the right thing to do at the time, but a serious commitment to ranching was in my future.

I had spent my summers helping out on my uncle's dairy farm, and then, as I got older, I'd go over and help him with milking. After a while I knew I didn't want to be in the dairy business, but I think that it is where my love of land and my love of cattle started.

Once I met Ruth, my high-school sweetheart, I was focused on playing sports, doing my best in school, and spending as much time with her as possible. She is a wonderful person and has been tremendously supportive of everything I've strived to achieve. She always enjoyed the cattle business, and has appreciated how much pleasure I get from being on ranches and spending time around livestock.

With all the factors that are out of your control in ranching and agriculture, I can honestly say that if you don't have passion and dedication, I don't see how you can stay with it. I have applied many of the same principles that guided me in baseball—focus, determination, and discipline—to my cattle operation.

In fact, I got back into the cattle business while I was pitching for the California Angels in 1973. I had been taking classes at Alvin Community College during the off-season, studying and reading up on cattle breeding and genetics. I was still living in Alvin, about an hour outside of Houston, and finally decided it was time to start a herd. George Pugh Sr., the father of a good friend, was retiring from working in the oil fields, and I knew that I could hire him to look after my cattle operation while I was pitching for the Angels.

Alvin used to be a big dairy farming community, but a lot of those dairy farmers switched over to raising beef cattle. One dairy had Jersey cows and bred them with a Brahman bull to create half-and-half Jersey-Brahman cows. Then they came back with a Hereford bull, and I felt that a three-way cross would be a good base cow, so I bought their heifers two years in a row.

The first piece of ranch property I bought in Gonzalez County dates all the way back to just after the Mets won the World Series in 1969. From that first ranch in 1970, we have been buying and building ranches for more than forty years. When a piece of land would come up that would work in our operation, we would try to acquire it, and then we would try to acquire anything that came up next to that, in order to amass as much contiguous land as we could.

WENDY: "I always thought of my dad as a cattle rancher. Our family would travel to cattle sales all over Texas and he would host auctions at our ranch. Spending time at our ranch was our most precious family time. We could get away from the routines of being in town and just enjoy being around the cows. I had a love for the ranch and the cattle business, and then I reached a point where I really didn't know what career path to follow after college. Dad asked me, "What do you love?" And I told him that I love the ranch more than anything. That's when I decided to make the ranch my job. I went to the Master's program in Ranch Management at Texas Christian University. It covered everything from learning about grasses for grazing to actually working the cattle and learning the cattle market. As soon as I got out of the program I went to work for my dad's ranch business and I worked to update the technology of the cattle business. My kids love spending time with their grandfather on the ranch and checking on the cows. It's a family passion that really spans all the generations."

RUTH: "Ever since I've known him he's had a passion for the cattle industry. He has always studied books about cattle and ranching. I knew he would stay in the business in some way."

Nowadays, our basic herd is Beefmaster cattle, an American breed that was started right here in Texas to survive and thrive in the arid heat. It is a three-way cross between the Brahman, the Hereford, and the Shorthorn. Then we cross them with either Red or Black Angus bulls. We also keep a purebred Beefmaster herd.

My success in baseball gave me the economic resources I needed to get started in the cattle business. I have taken the same measured, careful, and passionate approach to all my business operations, and buying and selling cattle and starting Nolan Ryan Beef have been no different.

When Charlie Bradbury first proposed lending my name to the Beefmaster brand of beef, I had to give the matter a lot of thought. At that point I knew nothing about the commercial end of the beef business. We brought in all the industry experts, from retail to meat science, for a two-day conference in San Antonio to debate the pros and cons. After much reflection and analysis we decided to move forward with the formation of Nolan Ryan Beef. Our goal has always been to produce the best beef products available from the best cattle.

My son Reese is a tremendous asset to the company. He has a good feel for the cattle business. He is also an astute adviser on all subjects about beef; he can see trends in the consumer market and understands the changes and shifts in the economy. In fact, all my kids have been a huge help to me in my various business endeavors. And my son Reid was promoted to the position of president of the Houston Astros, an achievement that makes me extremely proud.

REID: "Growing up, I always viewed my dad as both a cattle rancher and a baseball player. He would go to cattle auctions with us kids and teach us how to take care of cows, and we learned the business of being able to look five years down the road to figure out what a cow would develop into and how it would bring success to the family ranch business. That patience, bred in the cattle business, was a great boon to my dad in the baseball business as CEO of the Texas Rangers. He had the patience and vision to be able to look at the long-term picture, which is rare in baseball, a pitch-by-pitch business where most owners are focused on what a player is doing for you that day, that game.

Food has always been a big part of the Ryan family get-togethers. All the kids learned at a very young age how to behave at nice restaurants without making fools of ourselves. And when my dad came home during the off-season, the Sunday night cookout was a family tradition. My dad was (and is) an excellent grill chef, and he has always loved to cook steaks over charcoal to produce a great meal."

REESE: "Most people think of my father as one of the greatest power pitchers in the history of Major League Baseball; however, that's not exactly how I view him. To me, he has always been a cattleman as well as a baseball player. Our family spent most of the summer at the ballpark or traveling with the team during the baseball season, but the off-season meant family time with cattle auctions and hunting trips for deer, quail, and dove. Nolan was an avid hunter who taught me how to shoot and to respect wildlife, and I took great pleasure in that special feeling that came with growing up around cattle and learning to love those special times we cooked food outdoors, under the stars.

My sister Wendy and I followed in our father's footsteps with a love for the cattle business. We both attended the Texas Christian University Ranch Management graduate program, and this is where I learned about the processing and marketing of beef—a very different perspective on the industry. My dad's love of cattle ranching inspired us to work on his ranches, to help with buying and selling cattle, and to do whatever was necessary to make the cattle operation successful.

When my father decided to explore selling beef through the formation of Nolan Ryan Beef, I knew I wanted to help and joined the board of directors. But it is the personal side of my dad's love for cattle and the Western lifestyle that has had the greatest impact on me. I have passed along my passion for ranching, wildlife, and hunting to my family; my daughters, Caroline and Julia, and I go hunting with our friend and fellow cattle rancher Marjorie Bledsoe, who was raised working cattle and hunting in the 1930s.

Our entire family has been blessed by Nolan's passion for cattle ranching, and I am fortunate that I'm the son of a cattleman—and a great father."

Cooking over charcoal, mesquite, and hickory has always been one of my passions. I love the smoke-infused flavors that make a grilled T-bone, sirloin, or tenderloin something special. I am always working to take my flavors and techniques to another level. Growing up in Texas allowed me the chance to enjoy the regional flavors of the Southwest, and this style of cooking has become increasingly popular in the past twenty years.

In deciding to write this cookbook, I wanted to share my love for Texas barbecue and for grilling, roasting, pan-searing, and braising all cuts of beef. And I wanted to find a chef who could express and communicate the authentic southwestern and Mexican style of grilled-over-fire beef dishes of South Texas. I was fortunate to be able to enlist Cristobal Vazquez ("Chef Cris"), executive chef at the Rangers Ballpark in Arlington. The recipes we came up with are in some ways just the starting point on a journey of southwestern flavor: our goal is to liberate any chef to make good choices based on personal preferences, what's in the pantry, what's within the budget, and who is on the guest list for brunch, lunch, or dinner.

We worked together to create some seventy-five recipes that express my love of beef and cooking over fire in the great outdoors, and my passion for sharing these special dishes with friends and family.

Y'all enjoy!

A NOTE ON THE RECIPES

CRISTOBAL G. VAZQUEZ

Executive Chef, Texas Rangers Baseball

Working with Nolan Ryan to develop the recipes for this cookbook has been without a doubt the highlight of my career as a chef. I've had the pleasure to cook for Nolan and Ruth Ryan for the past five years, and through experimentation and improvisation I have learned to make the fresh, hearty, flavorful, and delicious food that they love.

We organized the book as a tour of the various cuts and preparations of beef, starting with a chapter of inventive burgers and sandwiches that capture the ballpark experience—taken to a higher level with the freshest ingredients and the flavors of the Southwest. Next come the cuts that work perfectly for grilling (indoors or outdoors), like rib-eye, T-bone, sirloin, and tenderloin. We then address Sunday roasts (some of Nolan's favorite family recipes) and regional specialties like beef ribs, brisket, and flank steaks that feature my special Tex-Mex spices. The journey concludes with classic side dishes, salads, and desserts, including Ruth Ryan's Special Occasion Carrot Cake.

Nolan and Ruth really appreciate good food. I talked to both of them almost every day to find out what they wanted to eat in "The Bunker," the private lounge where the Ryan family dined before each game while Nolan worked as CEO of the Texas Rangers. Nolan loves grilled T-bones, rib-eye carne asada, green bean casserole, and Sunday pot roast. Ruth enjoys the prime rib and, for dessert, my homemade flan with Tia Maria.

These recipes are based on Nolan's love for the Mexican and southwestern food of South Texas and my roots as a chef growing up in Aguascalientes, Mexico. This region of north-central Mexico is known for bullfighting, a state fair that attracts people from all over Mexico for its food, and the many beautiful hot springs from which my hometown derives its name.

Aguascalientes is the culinary home for enchiladas *verdes*, *carnitas* (crispy pork), *barbacoa* (meat cooked BBQ style), and carne asada. The food is fresh and honest. In Mexico, the concept of farm-to-table is nothing new. We have always prepared foods based on the local produce and meats to maximize freshness and flavor.

In crafting these recipes, we have integrated my love of Mexican ingredients such as guajillo peppers and Mexican chorizo (not cured like Spanish chorizo, but a fresh sausage that has to be cooked) with Nolan's appreciation for the simplicity and clarity of a beautiful grilled tenderloin or beef ribs cooked lovingly over charcoal.

Nolan, Ruth, and I want you to enjoy putting these recipes to the test at a Father's Day cookout with your friends and family, or at a special dinner when you'll discover that cooking prime rib is well worth the effort. We have given you simple, easy-to-follow instructions. And be on the lookout for Nolan's Tips—techniques for grilling and drawing out flavor as well as serving suggestions that can help you elevate every meal to something truly special.

Working with Nolan on this book has been a true pleasure. We hope you enjoy many wonderful meals from these recipes with your friends and family for years to come!

NOLAN RYAN'S GUIDE TO COOKING WITH BEEF

These guidelines are my go-to for preparing all of my dishes to perfection.

The cooking times in the charts that follow are those recommended by the National Cattlemen's Beef Association. Note that these are total cooking times (not per side) and should be considered general guidelines. Variances in specific makes and models of gas grills and ovens and the variability of charcoal cooking, depending on environmental factors and differences among types of wood and charcoal, will impact results. Take note of the suggested cooking times given within each recipe, but for best results, get to know your own grill setup. Following the charts are a few of my recommendations for buying, storing, and cooking beef, to get you headed in the right direction.

GRILLING

Here are my top five tips for great grilling:

- It's fine to take your beef right from the refrigerator to the grill—there's no need to bring the beef to room temperature.
- Always trim all visible fat before grilling to prevent flare-ups.
- Use a pair of metal tongs to turn roasts and steaks rather than a fork so you won't lose the delicious juices inside.
- High heat can char the exterior of the beef but leave the interior undercooked. Always use a meat thermometer to test the doneness of the meat.
- Have fun!

Gas Grilling

The guidelines in the chart on page 12 were based on the temperatures of a Weber Genesis gas grill set to medium heat, unless otherwise specified. Gas grill makes and models vary widely, so grilling times may need to be modified. Always carefully read your owner's manual for specific grilling instructions.

The cooking times in the charts range from medium-rare (145°F internal temperature) to medium (160°F).

Grilling with Charcoal

When coals become ash-covered, spread in a single layer and check cooking temperature by carefully cupping the palm of your hand above the coals at cooking height. Now, count the seconds it takes before the heat compels you to pull your hand away from the grill (it will take 4 seconds at medium heat, less for high).

GRILLING

	THICKNESS/WEIGHT	CHARCOAL COOKING TIME	GAS COOKING TIME
CHUCK			
Boneless Eye Chuck Steak	¾ inch	9–11 minutes	9–12 minutes
Shoulder Top Blade Steak (Flat Iron)	8 ounces	10–14 minutes	12–16 minutes
Shoulder Center Steak (Ranch)	¾ inch	8–11 minutes	8–11 minutes
Under Blade Center Steak (Denver Cut, boneless)	½ inch	4–7 minutes	5–8 minutes
RIB			
Rib Steak, small end	¾ inch 1 inch	7–10 minutes 10–15 minutes	7–10 minutes 10–15 minutes
Rib-Eye Steak	¾ inch 1 inch	7–10 minutes 10–14 minutes	7–9 minutes 9–14 minutes
LOIN			
Porterhouse/T-Bone Steak	¾ inch 1 inch	8–11 minutes 11–16 minutes	9–13 minutes 15–19 minutes
Boneless Top Loin Strip Steak	¾ inch	7–10 minutes	7–10 minutes
Tenderloin Steak	¾ inch 1 inch	7–10 minutes 10–14 minutes	7–10 minutes 11–15 minutes
SIRLOIN			
Boneless Top Sirloin Steak	¾ inch 1 inch	7–11 minutes 11–15 minutes	8–13 minutes 13–16 minutes
Tri-Tip Steak	¾ inch	8–10 minutes	8–10 minutes
ROUND (Nolan recommends cooking steaks from the round section to medium-rare, 145°F.)			
Round Sirloin Tip Center Steak	¾ inch	8–9 minutes	8–11 minutes
Round Sirloin Tip Side Steak	¾ inch	9–11 minutes	7–9 minutes
Bottom Round Steak	¾ inch	8–10 minutes	11–14 minutes
Top Round Steak	¾ inch	10–11 minutes	10–11 minutes
Eye of Round Steak	¾ inch	10–12 minutes	10–12 minutes
SKIRT AND FLANK			
Skirt Steak	1–1½ pounds	7–12 minutes	8–12 minutes
Flank Steak	1½–2 pounds	11–16 minutes	16–21 minutes
HAMBURGERS (Nolan recommends cooking hamburgers to at least medium, 160°F.)			
Beef patties	½ inch (4 ounces) ¾ inch (6 ounces)	8–10 minutes 11–15 minutes	7–9 minutes 13–14 minutes

PAN-SEARING

	THICKNESS/WEIGHT	COOKING TIME (ON MEDIUM)
CHUCK		
Boneless Eye Chuck Steak	¾ inch 1 inch	9–11 minutes 12–15 minutes
Shoulder Top Blade Steak (Flat Iron)	8 ounces	11–14 minutes
Shoulder Center Steak (Ranch)	¾ inch 1 inch	8–11 minutes 12–15 minutes
Under Blade Center Steak (Denver Cut, boneless)	½ inch (8 ounces)	3–4 minutes on medium-high
Blade Steak	1 inch	13–17 minutes
Boneless Shoulder Top Steak	¾ inch	11–13 minutes
Shoulder Petite Medium Medallions	½–¾ inch	4–6 minutes on medium-high
RIB		
Rib-Eye Steak	¾ inch 1 inch	8–11 minutes 12–15 minutes
LOIN		
Porterhouse/T-Bone Steak	¾ inch 1 inch	10–13 minutes 14–17 minutes
Boneless Top Loin Strip Steak	¾ inch 1 inch	8–11 minutes 12–15 minutes
Tenderloin Steak	½ inch ¾ inch 1 inch	3–5 minutes on medium-high 7–10 minutes 10–13 minutes
SIRLOIN		
Boneless Top Sirloin Steak	¾ inch 1 inch	12–15 minutes 15–18 minutes
Tri-Tip Steak	¾ inch 1 inch	9–12 minutes 10–13 minutes
ROUND (Nolan recommends cooking steaks from the round section to medium-rare, 145°F.)		
Round Sirloin Tip Center Steak	¾ inch 1 inch	11–13 minutes 14–15 minutes
Round Sirloin Tip Side Steak	¾ inch 1 inch	11–13 minutes 13–15 minutes
Bottom Round Steak	¾ inch 1 inch	11–14 minutes 16–22 minutes
Top Round Steak	¾ inch 1 inch	12–15 minutes 15–17 minutes
Eye of Round Steak	¾ inch 1 inch	8–10 minutes 11–13 minutes

BROILING

	THICKNESS/WEIGHT	DISTANCE FROM HEAT	COOKING TIME
CHUCK			
Shoulder Top Blade Steak (Flat Iron)	8 ounces	3–4 inches	15–20 minutes
Boneless Shoulder Steak	¾ inch 1 inch	2–3 inches 3–4 inches	10–13 minutes 16–21 minutes
RIB			
Rib Steak, small end	¾ inch	2–3 inches	9–12 minutes
Rib-Eye Steak	¾ inch 1 inch	2–3 inches 3–4 inches	8–10 minutes 14–18 minutes
LOIN			
Porterhouse/T-Bone Steak	¾ inch 1 inch	2–3 inches 3–4 inches	10–13 minutes 15–20 minutes
Boneless Top Loin Steak	¾ inch	2–3 inches	9–12 minutes
Strip Steak	1 inch	3–4 inches	13–17 minutes
Tenderloin Steak	1 inch	2–3 inches	13–16 minutes
SIRLOIN			
Boneless Top Sirloin Steak	¾ inch 1 inch 1½ inches 2 inches	2–3 inches 3–4 inches 3–4 inches 3–4 inches	9–11 minutes 16–21 minutes 26–31 minutes 34–39 minutes
ROUND (Nolan recommends cooking steaks from the round section to medium-rare, 145°F.)			
Top Round Steak	¾ inch 1 inch 1½ inches	2–3 inches 2–3 inches 3–4 inches	12–13 minutes 17–18 minutes 27–29 minutes
Bottom Round Steak	1¼ inches	3–4 inches	18–20 minutes
FLANK			
Flank Steak	1½–2 pounds	2–3 inches	13–18 minutes

Source: National Cattlemen's Beef Association

BRAISING

	THICKNESS/WEIGHT	COOKING TIME (COVERED, OVER LOW HEAT)
CHUCK		
Chuck Pot Roast	2½–4 pounds	2–3 hours
Boneless Shoulder Steak	¾–1 inch	1¼–2 hours
Short Ribs	2 by 2 by 4 inches	1½–2½ hours
ROUND		
Bottom Round Rump Roast (boneless)	3–4 pounds	2½–3¼ hours
Eye of Round Steak (boneless)	¾–1 inch 1–1½ inches	1¼–2 hours 2–2½ hours
BRISKET		
Fresh Brisket	2½–3½ pounds	2½–3 hours

Source: National Cattlemen's Beef Association

BUYING BEEF

The quality of the U.S. meat supply is regulated by the government. It is, in fact, the most highly regulated industry of its kind in the world, and all beef products must pass stringent inspections before being sold to the consumer.

The meat-grading program, for instance, is controlled by the U.S. Department of Agriculture (USDA). Beef grades reflect qualities such as tenderness and flavor, and these grades act as a guide to help you make intelligent choices about what you want to buy and how much money you want to spend. You'll find three grades of beef to choose from, and in the final analysis the decision is a matter of taste—for example, not everyone wants the kind of marbling that allows beef to be graded as USDA Prime. Here are the three grades and some explanation of how these grades are earned.

USDA Prime: This grade has the most marbling of fat and is sold to specialty meat markets and high-end restaurants such as Del Frisco's and Bob's Steak & Chop House in Fort Worth, Texas—among my personal favorites. USDA Prime is considered the best quality, but many people don't necessarily look for marbling of fat in their steak.

USDA Choice: Choice has less marbling than Prime, but is still a quality product. This is the beef you will find most easily in your local grocery store.

USDA Select: The least amount of marbling provides a leaner product, but with a little less flavor than Choice and Prime.

The Aging Process

The goal in aging beef is to tenderize it, particularly in loin and rib cuts. Most of the tenderization occurs in the first seven to ten days of the aging process, as this is when the natural enzymes in the beef break down the connective tissue in the fibers of the muscle. Dry and wet are the two techniques used to age beef.

Dry Aging: The beef is placed, uncovered, for up to twenty-eight days under refrigeration (32°F to 34°F) and in a humidity-controlled environment. Dry aging, though more expensive than wet aging, yields a rich and deep brown-roasted flavor to the meat.

Wet Aging: Wet aging improves tenderization and minimizes spoilage. The beef is aged in airtight sealed bags for up to twenty-one days under refrigeration (32°F to 34°F).

How to Decide What to Buy

The label will tell you what kind of meat it is, the wholesale cut, and the name of the cut. The label will also give you the weight, price per pound, total price, handling instructions, and the deadline for selling the beef to the consumer. In some cases, the label will also include preparation guidelines and the USDA grade. As for ground beef, the label will also indicate the lean-to-fat ratio (80 percent lean to 20 percent fat, for example) and the cut (sirloin, chuck, or round).

DETERMINING DONENESS

There is a surefire method for cooking your beef perfectly: I recommend that you buy both an instant-read thermometer and an oven-safe meat thermometer to guarantee that all your hard work and effort pay off with the best-tasting beef you have ever cooked.

Steaks: When cooking steaks (at least ½ inch thick), insert your instant-read thermometer horizontally from the side—it should penetrate the center part of the steak, not touching fat or bone. Here are the temperatures you're looking for, depending on the level of doneness you enjoy:

> **Medium-rare: 145°F**
>
> **Medium: 160°F**
>
> **Well-done: 170°F**

Roasts: Insert an oven-safe meat thermometer into the thickest part of the roast just prior to roasting, and leave it in for the entire roasting process. Or, if you are using an instant-read meat thermometer, insert it into the thickest part of the roast when you think the roast is done, and leave it in for 15 seconds (see the "Braising" chart on page 15 for temperature guidelines).

Ground Beef: Insert an instant-read thermometer into the center of a ground beef patty, meatballs, or a meatloaf. All ground beef should be cooked to an internal temperature of 160°F (medium doneness).

DEFROSTING & STORAGE GUIDELINES

Always defrost frozen beef in the refrigerator—never at room temperature. Place a plate under the meat to avoid making a mess. Use this chart as your blueprint for perfect timing.

DEFROSTING GUIDELINES		
BEEF CUT	**THICKNESS**	**REFRIGERATION TIME (35°F TO 40°F)**
Steaks, Ground Beef	½–¾ inch	12 hours
Kabobs/Skewers	1–1½ inches	24 hours
Small Roasts, Thin Pot Roasts	Variable	3–5 hours per pound
Large Roasts, Thick Pot Roasts	Variable	4–7 hours per pound

FREEZER & REFRIGERATOR STORAGE GUIDELINES (from purchase date)		
FRESH BEEF CUT	**FREEZER (0°F OR BELOW)**	**REFRIGERATOR (35°F TO 40°F)**
Roasts, Steaks	6 to 12 months	3 to 4 days
Kabobs/Skewers	6 to 12 months	2 to 3 days
Ground Beef	3 to 4 months	1 to 2 days

THE NOLAN RYAN BEEF & BARBECUE COOKBOOK

1

THE

BALLPARK EXPERIENCE

HAMBURGERS & HOT DOGS

NOLAN RYAN'S GRILLED AMERICAN BURGER

I am a hamburger purist, and that means that the ultimate Nolan Ryan burger is a well-done 80-20 ground chuck patty with lettuce, tomato, and spicy mustard. Over the years I have tried ketchup and mayonnaise, but I just don't care for those condiments on burgers. I do enjoy having the ground chuck cooked over smoke, but I'm not a fan of layering sauces on a hamburger, as it tends to hide the flavor of the meat. My approach is too basic for many people, so I worked with Chef Cris to take a classic hamburger and add the flavor combinations of sharp cheddar, smoke-infused bacon, and Montreal steak seasoning—a mix of salt, black pepper, paprika, garlic, onion, cayenne pepper, and coriander. The intensely flavored bacon and spice mix balance the richness of the cheese and the meat.

MAKES 8 BURGERS
PREP TIME: 20 MINUTES, PLUS 30 MINUTES TO CHILL THE MEAT
COOKING TIME: 10 MINUTES

---

4 slices bacon
4 pounds ground chuck (80-20 meat-to-fat-ratio)

4 ounces sharp cheddar cheese, shredded
¼ cup Montreal steak seasoning

4 large eggs, lightly beaten
8 hamburger buns, toasted

---

1 Preheat the oven to 350°F.

2 Cook the bacon on a baking sheet until crisp, about 15 minutes. Drain off the fat and pat the bacon dry with paper towels. Chop the bacon into very small (¹⁄₁₆-inch) pieces.

3 In a large bowl, combine the ground chuck, cheese, chopped bacon, seasoning, and eggs with a large serving fork and spatula. Finish mixing with your hands, but do not overmix.

4 Form the mixture into 8 patties and place on a parchment-lined baking sheet. The patties should be no more than ¾ inch thick or they will take too long to cook. Refrigerate the patties for 30 minutes to allow the seasoning to flavor the meat.

5 Preheat the grill or a grill pan to medium-high. If using a grill, lightly oil the grill grates.

6 Cook the patties (in batches, if necessary) for 5 minutes per side or until done to your liking.

7 Serve the patties on toasted buns.

BBQ KENTUCKY BOURBON BURGER

Simply garnished with caramelized onions and enhanced with Kentucky bourbon, this burger packs an incomparable, enormous flavor. This is the type of out-of-the-way offering that Ruth and I came to enjoy in "The Bunker," the owner's lounge at the Rangers Ballpark in Arlington. Kentucky bourbon is a versatile ingredient in both savory and sweet dishes, as it offers a unique dimension of flavor. In fact, one of the leading BBQ competitions in the world is the prestigious Jack Daniel's World Championship Invitational Barbecue, and some of the recipes created for the grilling section of this book are up to the rigors of any competition. You can find bourbon in sauces for steaks, burgers, ribs, pulled pork, and chicken, and even desserts like fried apples with bourbon caramel and pecan or walnut pie.

MAKES 8 BURGERS
PREP TIME: 25 MINUTES, PLUS 30 MINUTES TO CHILL THE MEAT
COOKING TIME: 6 TO 8 MINUTES

4 pounds ground chuck (80-20 meat-to-fat ratio)
1 cup Kentucky bourbon
2 tablespoons Worcestershire sauce
1 teaspoon liquid smoke
2 teaspoons kosher salt

1½ teaspoons ground cumin
1 teaspoon paprika
1 teaspoon freshly ground black pepper
1 tablespoon unsalted butter
1 tablespoon olive oil

3 large yellow onions, sliced thin
¼ cup chipotle barbecue sauce
8 ounces cheddar cheese, sliced
8 hamburger buns, toasted
2 large tomatoes, sliced

Nolan's Tip: The Kentucky bourbon sauce used in this recipe is superb, but keep in mind that quality ground chuck is still the star of the plate. Never let any sauce or condiment overwhelm the flavor of the beef.

1 Preheat the grill or a grill pan to medium-high. If using a grill, lightly oil the grill grates.

2 In a large bowl, combine the ground chuck, ⅔ cup of the bourbon, Worcestershire, liquid smoke, salt, cumin, paprika, and pepper and mix with a large serving fork and spatula. Finish mixing with your hands, but do not overmix.

3 Form the mixture into 8 patties and place on a parchment-lined baking sheet. The patties should be no more than ¾ inch thick or they will take too long to cook. Refrigerate the patties for 30 minutes to allow the seasonings to flavor the meat.

4 While the patties are setting up in the fridge, start the sauce. Heat the butter and oil in a large skillet over high heat. Add the onions and sauté until golden brown. Stir in the chipotle barbecue sauce and remaining ⅓ cup bourbon and reduce the heat to a simmer.

5 Cook the patties (in batches, if necessary) for 3 to 4 minutes per side for medium doneness.

6 Place a slice of cheese on top of each burger and cook until it melts, about a minute.

7 Place a burger on each bun bottom, top with sliced tomatoes, and finish with the onion-bourbon sauce. Cover with the bun tops and serve.

CAJUN BURGER

The cuisine of Louisiana gets its flavors from the collection of cooking traditions—Spanish, French, and African—from which it evolved. When you think of Cajun and Creole cooking, the dishes that come to mind are delicious étouffées, jambalayas, and gumbos. Ruth and I have really enjoyed our trips to Louisiana over the years, and the food is a big part of the experience. Chef Cris uses Cajun seasoning to make this burger something different from anything you have ever tried. I'm not a big fan of blue cheese, so I made it an optional part of the recipe, but feel free to add the blue cheese crumbles if you enjoy their sharp taste with your burger.

The best-known baseball player from Louisiana is probably Rusty Staub, a great left-handed hitter with the Houston Astros, Montreal Expos, and New York Mets. Rusty owned and cooked for several successful Cajun-style restaurants in New York City after he retired from baseball. He always enjoyed the regional food wherever he traveled during his big-league career, and I was very much the same, trying different local specialties and making the food of each city an important part of my baseball experience.

MAKES 8 BURGERS
PREP TIME: 20 MINUTES, PLUS 30 MINUTES TO CHILL THE MEAT
COOKING TIME: 10 MINUTES

4 slices bacon

4 pounds ground chuck (80-20 meat-to-fat ratio)

4 ounces (about 1 cup) blue cheese crumbles (optional)

¼ cup Cajun Spice Mix (recipe follows)

¼ cup Nolan Ryan Seasoning (recipe follows)

1 tablespoon seasoned salt

¼ cup yellow mustard

4 large eggs, lightly beaten

8 hamburger buns, toasted

1 Preheat the oven to 350°F.

2 Cook the bacon on a baking sheet until crisp, about 15 minutes. Drain off the fat and pat the bacon dry with paper towels. Chop the bacon into very small (¹⁄₁₆-inch) pieces.

3 In a large bowl, combine the ground chuck, blue cheese (if using), chopped bacon, seasonings, mustard, and eggs with a large serving fork and a spatula. Finish mixing with your hands, but do not overmix.

4 Form the mixture into 8 patties and place on a parchment-lined baking sheet. The patties should be no thicker than ¾ inch or they will take too long to cook. Refrigerate the patties for 30 minutes to allow the seasonings to flavor the meat.

5 Preheat the grill or a grill pan to medium-high. If using a grill, lightly oil the grill grates.

6 Cook the patties (in batches, if necessary) for 5 minutes per side or until done to your liking.

7 Serve the patties on toasted buns.

Nolan's Grilling Tip: Place the patties on the grill far enough apart for heat to circulate for even cooking.

Cajun Seasoning

Makes ½ cup
Prep time: 5 minutes

2 tablespoons kosher salt
1 tablespoon freshly ground black pepper
1 tablespoon cayenne pepper
1 tablespoon celery seed
1 tablespoon paprika
1 tablespoon onion powder
1 tablespoon garlic powder

Combine all of the ingredients in a small bowl. Store leftovers in an airtight container at room temperature.

Nolan Ryan Steak Seasoning

Makes about ½ cup
Prep time: 5 minutes

3 tablespoons kosher salt
3 tablespoons garlic powder
3 tablespoons paprika

Combine all of the ingredients in a small bowl. Store leftovers in an airtight container at room temperature.

SPICY CHORIZO BURGER WITH QUESO ASADERO

I grew up on Mexican food in Alvin, Texas, where there was an excellent local restaurant that served fresh, authentic, and inexpensive meals—and with a big family you can bet that the price of the meal was an important consideration for my parents. This grilled chorizo burger blends spicy sausage and ground chuck, and is part of the tradition of Tex-Mex cooking that's based on regional ingredients and distinct Mexican flavor combinations.

I have developed a taste for all types of southwestern regional interpretations of Mexican food, from Sonoran dishes in Arizona to the lighter and less spicy Baja style that is popular in southern California. When I pitched for the Angels I really enjoyed going out for fresh-cooked Mexican food when we'd have a day off, or on an evening when we'd had a day game—a rarity with the Angels.

MAKES 8 BURGERS
PREP TIME: 20 MINUTES, PLUS 30 MINUTES TO CHILL THE MEAT
COOKING TIME: 10 TO 14 MINUTES

½ cup Worcestershire sauce

1 tablespoon steak sauce of your choice

2 tablespoons vegetable oil

1 pound fresh Mexican chorizo

2 large yellow onions, thinly sliced

4 pounds ground chuck (80-20 meat-to-fat ratio)

1 pound asadero cheese, grated

Kosher salt and freshly ground black pepper

Outer leaves of 1 head iceberg lettuce

2 large tomatoes, sliced

8 hamburger buns, toasted

---

1 Preheat the grill or a grill pan to medium-high. If using a grill, lightly oil the grill grates.

2 Combine the Worcestershire and steak sauces in a small bowl and set aside.

3 In a cast-iron skillet, heat 1 tablespoon of the oil over medium-high heat and cook the chorizo until crisp. Drain off the fat and transfer the chorizo to a plate lined with paper towels; set aside.

4 In the same skillet, sauté the onions in the remaining tablespoon oil until golden brown. Keep warm over low heat.

5 Form the ground chuck into 16 patties. Place 8 of the patties on a baking sheet and top each with some chorizo and cheese. Place the other 8 patties on top of the cheese and chorizo; form a seal so that the sausage and cheese becomes a filling between the patties. Season the patties with salt and pepper to taste—go easy on the salt, as chorizo has a naturally high salt content. Refrigerate the patties for 30 minutes to allow the seasoning to flavor the meat.

6 Grill the burgers (in batches, if necessary) for 5 to 7 minutes per side for medium doneness; brush with the Worcestershire–steak sauce mixture while cooking.

7 Place lettuce leaves, tomato slices, burgers, and caramelized onions on the bottom burger buns. Top with the other half of the bun and enjoy.

SOUTHERN SURF & TURF BURGER WITH CILANTRO RÉMOULADE

The key consideration with shrimp, as with any seafood, is freshness. I'm not one to put a lot of effort into fighting with my food, though, so I want all of my seafood out of the shell and ready to eat. Lobster is not something I ever wasted much time over, and when I played against the Baltimore Orioles I was not interested in going out to the blue crab shacks, where they give you a mallet and an apron and you have to pound the shells into fragments and pick through the remains to enjoy the flavorful meat. I do love crabmeat, but I prefer to let someone else do the work. As for scallops, I like to pan-fry the smaller bay scallops, but I'll take shrimp over scallops any day of the week.

Chef Cris really went above and beyond in creating this recipe, as the cilantro rémoulade is the perfect complement to the flavors of the shrimp, char-grilled burger, Worcestershire sauce, and smoky bacon.

MAKES 8 BURGERS
PREP TIME: 30 MINUTES, PLUS 30 MINUTES TO CHILL THE MEAT
COOKING TIME: 8 TO 10 MINUTES

---

8 slices bacon

1 cup olive oil

¼ cup unsalted butter

1 teaspoon chopped garlic

2 pounds shrimp, peeled, deveined, and coarsely chopped

1 tablespoon kosher salt

1 tablespoon freshly ground black pepper

2 pounds ground chuck (80-20 meat-to-fat ratio)

2 tablespoons hot sauce

1 tablespoon Worcestershire sauce

¼ bunch cilantro, chopped (leaves only)

2 teaspoons Cajun Seasoning (page 25)

3 large eggs, lightly beaten

1 cup panko bread crumbs, plus more if needed

1 recipe Cilantro Rémoulade (recipe follows)

8 hamburger buns, toasted

Outer leaves from 1 head iceberg lettuce

2 large tomatoes, sliced

---

1 Preheat the oven to 325°F.

2 Place the bacon on a baking sheet and cook until partially done, 8 to 10 minutes. Transfer the bacon to a plate lined with paper towels and pat dry. Chop the bacon into very small (¹⁄₁₆-inch) pieces and set aside.

3 In a large sauté pan, heat 3 tablespoons of the olive oil over medium-high heat. Add the butter and stir to melt. Add the garlic, shrimp, salt, and pepper. Cook, stirring, until the shrimp is tender and pink, about 4 minutes—be careful not to overcook or the shrimp will become rubbery.

4 Remove the pan from the heat and set it aside to cool for 15 to 20 minutes.

5 In a large bowl, combine the beef, hot sauce, Worcestershire, cilantro, bacon, and Cajun seasoning. Add the cooled shrimp along with its cooking liquid, the eggs, and the bread crumbs, and mix with a spatula or large serving fork. Add more bread crumbs as needed if the mixture is too loose.

6 Form the mixture into 8 patties and place on a parchment-lined baking sheet. The patties should be no more than ¾ inch thick or they will take too long to cook. Refrigerate the patties for 30 minutes to allow the seasoning to flavor the meat.

7 In a large sauté pan over medium-high heat, heat the rest of the oil. Once the oil is hot, cook the patties (in batches, if necessary) for 4 to 5 minutes per side for medium doneness.

8 Pat the cooked burgers with a paper towel.

9 Spread some cilantro rémoulade on both the top and bottom hamburger buns. Place some lettuce and tomato on each bun bottom, top with a burger, cover with the bun tops, and serve.

Cilantro Rémoulade

Makes 1½ cups
Prep time: 10 minutes

1 cup mayonnaise
1½ teaspoons chopped red onion
1 teaspoon pickle relish
Juice of 2 lemons
½ teaspoon chopped capers
¼ bunch cilantro, chopped (leaves only)
1 teaspoon hot sauce
Kosher salt and freshly ground black pepper to taste

Combine all of the ingredients in a small bowl. Cover and chill until ready to use.

SPICY BAJA BLT BURGER WITH CILANTRO RÉMOULADE

I decided to use whole-grain bread for this recipe to make it eat more like a typical BLT sandwich, although when you're grilling outdoors over charcoal you can easily toast a classic hamburger bun to handle what is admittedly a very big burger. The inclusion of mushrooms and avocado is a curveball that will really please your guests. I love mushrooms; they are an underutilized ingredient in grilling burgers, and they add a touch of earthy flavor. Chef Cris uses an herbal sauce (cilantro rémoulade) in place of the standard mayonnaise you'd find on a BLT.

MAKES 8 BURGERS
PREP TIME: 30 MINUTES, PLUS 30 MINUTES TO CHILL THE MEAT
COOKING TIME: 12 MINUTES

16 slices applewood-smoked bacon
2 tablespoons olive oil
8 ounces white mushrooms, sliced
1 tablespoon balsamic vinegar
1 tablespoon honey
4 pounds ground chuck (80-20 meat-to-fat ratio)

1 teaspoon Nolan Ryan Steak Seasoning (page 25)
8 slices Swiss cheese
16 slices whole-grain bread or 8 whole-wheat hamburger buns, toasted

1 cup Cilantro Rémoulade (page 29)
Outer leaves from 1 head red or green leaf lettuce
2 tomatoes, sliced thin
2 red onions, sliced thin
2 large avocados, peeled, pitted, and sliced thin

1 Preheat the grill or a grill pan to medium-high and the oven to 400°F. If using a grill, lightly oil the grill grates.

2 Cook the bacon on a baking sheet in the oven until crisp, about 15 minutes. Drain off the fat, pat the bacon dry with paper towels, and tent with foil to keep warm. Leave the oven on.

3 Meanwhile, in a medium sauté pan, heat the olive oil over medium heat. Sauté the mushrooms until tender. Transfer the mushrooms to a bowl and add the balsamic and honey; stir to combine and then set aside at room temperature.

4 Form the ground chuck into 8 patties. Season the burgers with the steak seasoning. Refrigerate the patties for 30 minutes to allow the seasoning to flavor the meat.

5 Grill the burgers (in batches, if necessary) for 6 minutes per side for medium-well.

6 Place the burgers on a baking sheet and top with the bacon, mushrooms, and cheese; bake for a few minutes until the cheese melts.

7 Spread some cilantro rémoulade on all of the toast slices. Place some lettuce, tomato, onion, and avocado on half of the toast slices. Top each with a burger, cover with the remaining toast slices, and serve.

Nolan's Grilling Tip: After forming the burger patties, it's a good idea to put them in the refrigerator for a half hour or so to let them firm up. This will also help enhance the flavor by letting all of the ingredients soak into the patty before grilling.

CHILE RELLENO BURGER WITH ROASTED SALSA ROJA

I really enjoy a good chile relleno. Here Chef Cris combines the rich flavors of poblano peppers with the delicious smokiness of grilled beef and mild sliced avocado. My son Reid and his wife, Nicole, absolutely love Mexican food, and this dish is right up their alley. As for me, the red salsa really makes this burger something special. I always prefer a good red salsa to a green salsa because the salsa *roja* has more depth—but they both have a place in healthy, authentic southwestern cooking.

MAKES 8 BURGERS
PREP TIME: 20 MINUTES, PLUS 30 MINUTES TO CHILL THE MEAT
COOKING TIME: 12 MINUTES

---

4 poblano peppers
½ cup Worcestershire sauce
1 tablespoon steak sauce of your choice
4 pounds ground chuck (80-20 meat-to-fat ratio)

1 pound asadero or provolone cheese, shredded
1 teaspoon Nolan Ryan Steak Seasoning (page 25)
8 hamburger buns, toasted

Outer leaves from 1 head iceberg lettuce
2 large tomatoes, sliced
3 avocados, peeled, pitted, and sliced thin
1 recipe Salsa *Roja* (page 37)

---

1 Preheat the grill or a grill pan to medium-high. If using a grill, lightly oil the grill grates.

2 Roast the poblano peppers on the grill or stovetop until nicely charred. Put the peppers in a plastic bag and cool them down in the refrigerator for 10 minutes to sweat them. Cut the peppers in half, remove the seeds, and peel off the skin.

3 Combine the Worcestershire and steak sauces in a small bowl and set aside.

4 Form the ground chuck into 16 patties. Place 8 patties on a baking sheet; top each with half of a poblano and some shredded cheese. Place the other 8 patties on top of the pepper and cheese and form a seal so that the pepper and cheese becomes a filling between the patties. Season the burgers on both sides with the steak seasoning. Refrigerate the patties for 30 minutes to allow the seasoning to flavor the meat.

5 Grill the patties (in batches, if necessary) for 6 minutes per side for medium-well; brush with the Worcestershire–steak sauce mixture with each turn.

6 Top each bottom burger bun with lettuce, tomato, and avocado. Place a burger on top and cover with the bun tops. Serve with salsa *roja* on the side.

GOURMET ONION BURGER WITH PORT WINE SAUCE

I really appreciate the port wine in the sauce for this burger, and I have seen port used effectively with a variety of preparations for grilled steaks. Vic & Anthony's Steakhouse, a restaurant located near Minute Maid Park in Houston, serves a port peppercorn sauce for its superb filet mignon. Port is one of those ingredients that adds something special to the flavor of the beef. With this dish, though, the crunchy onions are still the star ingredient.

With this recipe the key is to brush the burgers with the combination of Worcestershire, steak sauce, and port before and during grilling.

MAKES 8 BURGERS
PREP TIME: 10 MINUTES, PLUS 30 MINUTES TO CHILL THE MEAT
COOKING TIME: 10 TO 12 MINUTES

---

4 pounds ground chuck (80-20 meat-to-fat ratio)
1½ teaspoons kosher salt
1 teaspoon freshly ground black pepper

2 teaspoons Worcestershire sauce
1 cup steak sauce of your choice
2 teaspoons port
8 hamburger buns, toasted

2 (6-ounce) packages French-fried onions
Mustard of your choice

Nolan's Tip: The ideal burger should be 80-20—that is, 80 percent beef to 20 percent fat—and cooked over medium-high heat to give it a nice char.

1 Preheat the grill or a grill pan to medium-high. If using a grill, lightly oil the grill grates.

2 Form the ground chuck into 8 patties and season with salt and pepper. The patties should be no thicker than ¾ inch or they will take too long to cook. Refrigerate the patties for 30 minutes to allow the seasoning to flavor the meat.

3 In a medium bowl, combine the Worcestershire, steak sauce, and port; brush the burgers with this sauce before putting them on the grill.

4 Cook the patties (in batches, if necessary) for 5 to 6 minutes per side for medium-well, basting with the sauce with each turn.

5 Place a burger on each bun bottom, top with fried onions and mustard, and cover with the bun tops.

FIESTA BEEF SLIDERS WITH PICO DE GALLO

Offered as an appetizer on most Texas restaurant menus, between the fried chicken tenders and carne asada quesadillas, this dish gets its punch of Southwest flavor from *pico de gallo*—a delicious blend of red onions, fresh tomatoes, cilantro, and jalapeño peppers.

I'm providing instructions both for making homemade sliders and for using Nolan Ryan Beef pre-cooked sliders, which can be baked in the oven and then finished over charcoal, if you like, to give them that cookout flavor. Sliders make for a lean and tasty high-protein snack, so it's not surprising that they're one of the fastest growing food trends in the United States.

MAKES 16 SLIDERS
PREP TIME: 10 MINUTES, PLUS 30 MINUTES TO SEASON THE MEAT
COOKING TIME: 6 TO 15 MINUTES

Homemade Sliders

2 pounds ground chuck (80-20 meat-to-fat ratio)
1 teaspoon kosher salt
1 teaspoon freshly ground black pepper
1 tablespoon Worcestershire sauce
16 slider buns, toasted
4 avocados, peeled, pitted, and sliced thin
1 recipe Pico de Gallo (recipe follows)

1 In a large bowl, combine the ground chuck, salt, pepper, and Worcestershire with a large fork and spatula. Finish mixing with your hands, but do not overmix.

2 Form the mixture into 16 sliders, or mini burger patties, and place on a parchment-lined baking sheet. Refrigerate the patties for 30 minutes to allow the seasonings to flavor the meat.

3 Preheat the grill or a grill pan to medium-high. If using a grill, lightly oil the grill grates.

4 Cook the patties (in batches, if necessary) for 3 to 4 minutes per side.

5 Place a slider on each slider bun bottom, top with avocado and *pico de gallo*, and cover with the bun tops.

Nolan Ryan's Beef Sliders

16 Nolan Ryan Beef pre-cooked sliders, thawed
16 slider buns, toasted
4 avocados, peeled, pitted, and sliced thin
1 recipe Pico de Gallo (recipe follows)

1 Preheat the oven to 375°F.

2 Place the Nolan Ryan sliders on a well-oiled baking sheet. Bake the sliders for 12 to 15 minutes (following the cooking directions on the package). If you have a grill at the ready, finish for 1 minute per side on the grill for extra char.

3 Place a slider on each slider bun bottom, top with avocado and *pico de gallo*.

Pico de Gallo

Makes about 2 cups
Prep time: 10 minutes

2 medium red onions, diced
2 to 3 medium tomatoes, diced
2 jalapeño peppers, seeded and diced small
½ bunch fresh cilantro, chopped (leaves only)
Juice of 2 limes
1½ teaspoons kosher salt
1 teaspoon freshly ground black pepper

Combine all of the ingredients in a medium bowl. Cover and chill until ready to use.

BREAKFAST BURGER ON TEXAS TOAST WITH SALSA ROJA

Texas toast is a rich and savory side dish that Texas-style cafes introduced before toasters became popular. The thick, buttered white bread is seasoned and placed on a grill until it turns golden brown. Texas toast has been popularized in the Southwest by Dairy Queen, and I have to admit that I have from time to time ordered a single piece of Texas toast at the drive-through window at DQ to get me through to dinner without spoiling my appetite.

Think of this creative dish as the southwestern cousin to the standard breakfast sandwich—those bacon-and-egg classics you now find on every breakfast menu in America. In what I would call a Mexican brunch-at-the-ballpark item, this merging of ground chuck, hash-brown potatoes, bacon, and eggs is the perfect topping for a rich bottom layer of delicious (and classic) Texas toast.

MAKES 4 BURGERS
PREP TIME: 45 MINUTES, PLUS 30 MINUTES TO CHILL THE MEAT
COOKING TIME: 8 TO 10 MINUTES

8 slices bacon
1 pound ground chuck (80-20 meat-to-fat ratio)
Kosher salt and freshly ground black pepper to taste
½ cup plus 2 tablespoons olive oil or vegetable oil

1 pound small potatoes (preferably Yukon Gold), coarsely chopped
8 large eggs
8 slices Texas Toast (recipe follows)
4 slices mild cheddar cheese
4 slices pepper jack cheese

4 slices red onion
4 slices tomato
4 slices avocado
1½ cups Salsa *Roja* (recipe follows)
Hot sauce

1 Preheat the oven to 350°F.

2 Cook the bacon in a medium skillet over medium-high heat until crisp. Transfer the bacon to a plate lined with paper towels and set aside at room temperature.

3 Form the ground chuck into 4 patties. The patties should be no thicker than ¾ inch or they will take too long to cook. Season the patties with salt and pepper. Refrigerate the patties for 30 minutes to allow the seasoning to flavor the meat.

4 Heat ¼ cup of the oil in a large cast-iron skillet or heavy sauté pan over medium-high heat. Cook the patties (in batches, if necessary) for 4 to 5 minutes per side. Transfer the burgers to a plate and tent with foil to keep warm.

5 Heat ¼ cup of the oil in the same skillet over medium-high heat. Add the potatoes and season with salt and pepper. Cook, gently turning, until the potatoes are golden brown all over, about 4 minutes. Set the pan aside and cover to keep warm.

6 Heat the remaining 2 tablespoons olive oil in a nonstick pan over medium-high heat. Cook 2 eggs at a time, 2 minutes per side, until all 8 eggs are cooked "over hard."

7 Place 4 slices of the Texas toast on a baking sheet. Top each slice with 1 burger, 2 eggs, one-quarter of the potatoes, 2 slices of bacon, 1 slice of cheddar cheese, and 1 slice of pepper jack cheese and pop it in the oven until the cheese is melted.

8 Remove from the oven and add 1 slice of onion, 1 slice of tomato, and 1 slice of avocado to each burger. Cover with the remaining 4 slices of Texas toast.

9 Serve with salsa *roja* and hot sauce on the side.

Texas Toast

Makes 10 to 12 slices
Prep time: 5 minutes
Cooking time: 5 minutes

1 cup (½ pound) salted butter, melted
6 garlic cloves, minced
1 teaspoon ground cumin
1 teaspoon kosher salt
1 teaspoon freshly ground black pepper
2 loaves good-quality white bread, sliced thick

1 Preheat the grill to high.

2 Mix the butter and garlic in a small bowl and season with the cumin, salt, and pepper.

3 Brush both sides of the bread with the garlic butter.

4 Grill the bread until golden brown, about 2 minutes per side.

Salsa Roja (Roasted Tomato Salsa)

Makes about 2 cups
Prep time: 20 minutes

8 large Roma tomatoes, halved lengthwise
4 jalapeño peppers, stemmed and halved lengthwise
4 garlic cloves, peeled
½ small white onion, cut into chunks
1 tablespoon olive oil or vegetable oil
½ cup chicken broth
Juice of 1 lime
1 teaspoon adobo sauce (from a can of chipotle peppers in adobo sauce)
½ bunch fresh cilantro (leaves only)
1 teaspoon kosher salt
1 teaspoon freshly ground black pepper

1 Preheat the oven to 425°F.

2 Spread out the tomatoes, jalapeños, garlic cloves, and onion chunks on a baking sheet. Drizzle with the olive oil and toss gently with your hands to mix.

3 Roast the vegetables until golden brown, about 15 minutes.

4 Transfer the roasted vegetables to a blender and add the chicken broth, lime juice, and adobo sauce. Blend on low speed for 3 to 5 seconds. Add the cilantro, salt, and pepper and blend for another 3 to 5 seconds. The salsa should be chunky, so don't overblend.

5 Serve the salsa hot, or cover and refrigerate to serve cold.

Nolan's Tip: Feel free to substitute this red salsa for the green salsa in any recipe that calls for a salsa *verde*. Texas-style Mexican cooking is based on red salsa, not green, and that's what I generally prefer.

TEX-MEX TACO DOG

Taco sauce, as it relates to southwestern cooking, means **different** things to different people. Cris and I agree that you don't put beans in taco sauce. Texans grow up with the rule that you don't put beans in your chili—and that rule applies to the ground beef–based taco sauce that makes this hot dog the go-to item at any party or BBQ. A good chili can include kidney beans only if it also has onions and tomato paste. My son Reese is the chili chef in our family, and his chili really stands out for its smoke, depth of flavor, and perfectly cooked ground chuck.

MAKES 8 HOT DOGS
PREP TIME: 5 MINUTES
COOKING TIME: 15 MINUTES

8 all-beef hot dogs
8 hot dog buns
8 hard taco shells
1 recipe Taco Sauce (recipe follows)

½ head iceberg lettuce, shredded
2 cups Pico de Gallo (page 34)
8 ounces cheddar cheese, shredded
½ cup sliced pickled jalapeños

½ cup sour cream
1 cup Salsa Roja (page 37)

1 Preheat the grill to medium-high and lightly oil the grill grates.

2 Slit the hot dogs lengthwise, halfway through, and grill them for 6 to 8 minutes, turning frequently.

3 Toast the buns and the taco shells on the grill.

4 Place a taco shell inside each bun and a hot dog inside the taco shell, and top with taco sauce, lettuce, *pico de gallo*, cheese, and jalapeños.

5 Serve with sour cream and salsa *roja* on the side.

Taco Sauce

Makes about 3 cups
Prep time: 5 minutes
Cooking time: 20 minutes

1 tablespoon vegetable oil
½ cup chopped onion
1 pound ground chuck (80-20 meat-to-fat ratio)
1 teaspoon chili powder
1 teaspoon paprika
¾ teaspoon kosher salt
½ teaspoon garlic powder
1 cup tomato juice

1 Heat the oil in a large sauté pan over high heat and cook the onions until golden brown. Add the ground chuck, stirring until crumbly, and then add the chili powder, paprika, salt, and garlic powder. Cook, stirring, until the meat is no longer pink, about 5 minutes.

2 Drain off the excess fat and add the tomato juice. Reduce the heat to low and cook the meat, stirring, until the juices almost dry up.

3 Remove the pan from the heat and cover to keep warm until ready to serve.

TEXAS RANGER DOG WITH BACON, PICO DE GALLO, GREEN RELISH & SAUTÉED ONIONS

I grew up eating grilled hot dogs with yellow mustard and green relish on a classic hot dog bun. But Chef Cris came up with a very popular recipe that combines the salty, smoke-infused flavor of slab bacon and the fresh flavors of *pico de gallo* and sautéed onions. The onions, relish, and yellow mustard add tang and depth, and this is an easy-to-prepare crowd pleaser on game day.

When I was pitching for the Houston Astros I'd always go out of my way to enjoy a Dodger Dog every time we played in Los Angeles. Vin Scully, the legendary Dodgers' broadcaster, pitched Farmer John Dodger Dogs on his pregame show; he was so passionate about them that he convinced us all that they were the greatest hot dogs on earth!

One of the great things about baseball is that the longer the game, the more food you get to enjoy at the ballpark. My games were a little longer because I threw a lot of pitches. The funny thing about my career is that people talk about my seven no-hitters as my greatest achievement, but I never consciously thought about no-hitters. I'd rather win 5–4 than lose 1–0 with sixteen strikeouts. You can't put personal goals ahead of your team.

MAKES 12 HOT DOGS
PREP TIME: 5 MINUTES
COOKING TIME: 20 MINUTES

---

24 slices bacon
12 all-beef hot dogs
1 tablespoon vegetable oil

2 large yellow onions, sliced
12 hot dog buns, toasted
Green relish

Yellow mustard
1½ cups Pico de Gallo (page 34)

---

1 Preheat the oven to 350°F.

2 Wrap 2 bacon slices around each hot dog. Cook the hot dogs on a baking sheet for 15 minutes. Reserve the bacon drippings.

3 Finish the hot dogs in a large skillet over medium heat until the bacon is crisp, and then transfer to a plate. (You can also finish the hot dogs on a grill heated to medium.)

4 Add the reserved bacon fat and the vegetable oil to the skillet and sauté the onions until golden brown.

5 Place the hot dogs in buns and top with onions, relish, and yellow mustard.

6 Serve the *pico de gallo* on the side.

2

T-BONES, RIB-EYE STEAKS

& STRIP STEAKS

BIG TEX RIB-EYE WITH ADOBO BUTTER

Boneless rib-eye steaks are delicious because the marbling adds a rich, complex flavor. I believe that the bone-in rib-eye craze is a gimmick for restaurants to make a greater profit on selling beef to the consumer. You will find that the flavor in the rib-eye is in the meat—not in the bone. I don't buy the hype that the bone adds even more flavor.

Chef Cris recommends you serve the Big Tex Rib-Eye with Adobo Butter over a generous portion of his famous Garlic Mashed Potatoes (page 138). I especially enjoy the flavor of the potatoes once they absorb some of the juices of the steak.

SERVES 8
PREP TIME: 10 MINUTES, PLUS 1 HOUR TO MARINATE THE MEAT
COOKING TIME: 6 TO 8 MINUTES

¼ cup Worcestershire sauce

2 tablespoons chopped garlic

8 (10- to 12-ounce) boneless rib-eye steaks, 1 inch thick

1 to 2 tablespoons chipotle peppers in adobo sauce

1 cup (½ pound) unsalted butter, at room temperature

1 teaspoon kosher salt

1 teaspoon freshly ground black pepper

1 Combine the Worcestershire and garlic in a large glass baking dish and add the steaks, turning to coat well. Cover and place the steaks in the refrigerator to marinate for 1 hour.

2 Chop the chipotle peppers and combine the peppers and adobo sauce with the softened butter in a small bowl. Stir well to blend. Cover and place the adobo butter in the fridge or freezer to firm up.

3 Preheat the grill or a grill pan to high. If using a grill, lightly oil the grill grates.

4 Remove the steaks from the marinade and season them with salt and pepper. Cook the steaks (in batches, if necessary) for 3 to 4 minutes per side for medium-rare.

5 Remove the steaks from the grill and let them rest on a platter for 5 minutes.

6 Top each steak with a dollop of adobo butter just before serving.

PAN-FRIED HERB-CRUSTED RIB-EYE

In this recipe, we marry the big flavors of a rib-eye with a delicious crust of oregano, cilantro, and smoked paprika, and then pan-fry the steak. Growing up in Alvin, Texas, pan-frying meat was a common and very simple preparation. Rib-eye performs perfectly in recipes like this because its rich marbling of fat adapts well to herbs, and it sears to perfection in a hot pan with olive oil.

SERVES 8
PREP TIME: 15 MINUTES
COOKING TIME: 10 TO 20 MINUTES

¼ cup chopped fresh oregano
¼ cup chopped fresh cilantro
1 tablespoon chopped, seeded jalapeños
½ cup ground cumin
½ cup smoked paprika

1 teaspoon kosher salt, plus more to season the sauce
8 (8- to 10-ounce) boneless rib-eye steaks
¼ cup olive oil
3 cups beef broth

½ cup dry sherry
½ cup honey
½ cup (¼ pound) unsalted butter, chilled and cut into pieces
Freshly ground black pepper

1 In a small bowl, combine the oregano, cilantro, jalapeños, cumin, paprika, and salt to make a spice mixture.

2 Sprinkle the steaks on both sides with about two-thirds of the spice mixture, reserving the remainder to add to the sauce.

3 Heat the oil in a large cast-iron skillet over medium heat.

4 Cook the steaks (in batches, if necessary) for 5 to 10 minutes per side (about 5 minutes for medium-rare and about 10 minutes for medium).

5 Transfer the steaks to a platter and set aside. Tent with foil to keep warm.

6 In the same skillet, combine the broth, sherry, honey, and the remaining spice mixture. Bring to a boil, then reduce the heat and let simmer for 3 to 5 minutes.

7 Remove the skillet from the heat and whisk in the chilled butter. Season the sauce to taste with salt and pepper.

8 Pour the sauce over the steaks and serve.

Nolan's Serving Tip: I like to serve this steak with Potatoes au Gratin (page 134) and a vegetable.

GRILLED CARNE ASADA TORTILLAS WITH SALSA VERDE & QUESO

This dish was originally planned for the chapter on flank steak, but I told Chef Cris I would rather go with a carne asada made with rib-eye because it has so much more flavor than a flank steak. Cris has provided an excellent salsa *verde* recipe to serve with this dish, but you can substitute his salsa *roja* if you prefer (see the recipe on page 37). The astonishingly delicious carne asada, well seasoned with the onions, lemon juice, and tequila, is spicy (but not too spicy) because of the charred banana peppers.

SERVES 8
PREP TIME: 20 MINUTES, PLUS 1 HOUR TO MARINATE THE MEAT
COOKING TIME: 6 TO 8 MINUTES

2 large yellow onions, sliced
¼ cup tequila
1 tablespoon fresh lemon juice
2 tablespoons vegetable oil
1 teaspoon kosher salt

2 pounds boneless rib-eye steaks, ½ inch thick
6 fresh banana peppers
16 flour tortillas
1 bunch fresh cilantro, chopped (leaves only)

8 ounces *queso fresco*, crumbled, or pepper jack cheese, sliced
2 limes, cut into wedges
1 recipe Salsa Verde (recipe follows)

1 Place one-quarter of the onions, the tequila, the lemon juice, 1 tablespoon of the oil, and the salt in a large glass baking dish. Add the meat, cover, and marinate in the refrigerator for at least 1 hour.

2 Preheat the grill to medium-high and lightly oil the grill grates.

3 Heat the remaining 1 tablespoon vegetable oil in a medium skillet and cook the remaining onions until golden brown; set aside.

4 Char the banana peppers on the grill, slice, and keep warm.

5 Remove the steaks from the marinade and grill the steaks (in batches, if necessary) for 3 to 4 minutes per side for medium-rare. Let the meat rest for 5 minutes and then slice thin.

6 Wrap the tortillas in foil and warm them quickly on the grill.

7 Assemble the soft tacos with the steak in the middle of the tortilla, then the caramelized onions, cilantro, banana peppers, and cheese.

8 Serve with lime wedges and salsa *verde*.

Salsa Verde

Makes about 2 cups
Prep time: 20 minutes

1 pound tomatillos, husked
2 jalapeño peppers, seeded and minced
2 garlic cloves, peeled
2 cups water
½ bunch fresh cilantro, chopped (leaves only)
1 teaspoon chopped fresh oregano
½ teaspoon ground cumin
1 pinch kosher salt

1 In a large skillet or on a grill, char the tomatillos, jalapeños, and garlic cloves.

2 Bring the water to a boil in a medium saucepan over high heat and add the tomatillos, jalapeños, and garlic cloves.

3 Reduce the heat to medium and simmer until the tomatillos are soft, 8 to 10 minutes.

4 Transfer the contents of the saucepan to a blender, add the cilantro, oregano, cumin, and salt, and puree for a few seconds. This salsa can be chunky or smooth, however you like it.

5 Transfer the salsa to a bowl, cover, and place in the fridge until ready to serve.

BLACKENED RIB-EYE STEAK SANDWICHES WITH BISTRO DRESSING

The best lunch you've ever had? Try this cooked-over-charcoal rib-eye with a wonderful dressing of Dijon mustard and mayonnaise. I like my steak sandwiches served on toasted whole-grain bread with lettuce and sliced tomato and avocado. They go great with Chef Cris's Loaded Yukon Gold Smashed Potatoes (page 137).

SERVES 8
PREP TIME: 5 MINUTES
COOKING TIME: 8 TO 10 MINUTES

8 (6- to 8-ounce) rib-eye steaks, ½ inch thick
2 tablespoons Cajun Seasoning (page 25)
1 teaspoon kosher salt
1 teaspoon freshly ground black pepper
16 slices whole-grain bread
8 slices white cheddar cheese
Outer leaves of 1 head iceberg lettuce
2 large tomatoes, sliced thin
1 red onion, sliced thin
4 avocados, peeled, pitted, and sliced thin
1 recipe Bistro Dressing (recipe follows)

Nolan's Tip: If you barbecue a rib-eye and are for some reason faced with leftovers (a rarity in the Ryan family), the next day's steak sandwiches are a treat.

1 Preheat the grill to medium-high and lightly oil the grill grates.

2 Season the steaks with the Cajun seasoning, salt, and pepper.

3 Grill the steaks (in batches, if necessary) for 4 to 5 minutes per side for medium-rare.

4 Remove the steaks from the grill and transfer to a cutting board; let the meat rest for 5 minutes.

5 Place the bread on the still-warm grill until golden brown.

6 Cut the steaks diagonally across the grain into thin strips.

7 Construct each sandwich with the steak on the bottom slice of bread, topped with cheese, lettuce, tomato, red onion, and avocado. Spread some dressing on the top slice of bread before closing it.

Bistro Dressing

Makes about ⅔ cup
Prep time: 5 minutes

½ cup mayonnaise
2 tablespoons Dijon mustard
Kosher salt and freshly ground black pepper

In a small bowl, combine the mayonnaise and mustard. Add salt and pepper to taste.

RIB-EYE WITH SRIRACHA-SOY MARINADE

With this recipe I marinate the rib-eye in a mixture of soy sauce, sriracha hot sauce, honey, garlic, ginger, mustard powder, scallion, and pineapple juice, mixing and crushing the ingredients and squeezing them to release maximum flavor. Marinate the steaks for at least 2 hours for best results.

SERVES 8
PREP TIME: 15 MINUTES, PLUS 2 HOURS TO MARINATE THE MEAT
COOKING TIME: 10 TO 14 MINUTES

1 cup soy sauce
1 cup dark beer
¼ cup honey
¼ cup pineapple juice
10 garlic cloves, minced

½ bunch scallions, chopped
2 tablespoons grated fresh ginger
2 tablespoons sriracha hot sauce
2 tablespoons mustard powder

1 teaspoon toasted sesame oil
8 (8- to 10-ounce) rib-eye steaks, 1 inch thick
1 large yellow onion, cut in half

1 In a medium bowl, combine all of the ingredients except the steaks and onion; mix well.

2 With a paring knife, punch holes in the rib-eye steaks. Place 4 steaks in each of two large zip-top bags and add half of the marinade mixture to each bag. Press the air out of the bags and seal.

3 Put the bags with the meat in the fridge for a minimum of 2 hours.

4 Preheat the grill to high. Lightly oil the grill grates.

5 Using a large fork, rub the grill with the cut sides of the onion halves for a sweet, smoky flavor.

6 Remove the steaks from the marinade. Grill the steaks (in batches, if necessary) for 5 to 7 minutes per side for medium-rare. Remove the steaks from the grill and let them rest on a platter for 5 minutes.

Nolan's Grilling Tip: Press the meat as required during the cooking process with a foil-wrapped brick to maintain contact with the grill. Baste with a brush and flip the steaks as needed.

Nolan's Serving Tip: I enjoy this steak with my Potatoes au Gratin (page 134).

GRILLED T-BONE WITH BOURBON-PEPPERCORN SAUCE

This is a new take on a peppercorn steak; the addition of butter and lemon juice is the perfect foil to the intensity of the peppercorns. The touch of bourbon has the same flavor impact as the port wine in the port-peppercorn sauce that is offered at Vic & Anthony's Steakhouse, next to Minute Maid Park, where the Astros play.

When I signed a free-agent deal with the Houston Astros, my goal was to prove that I could be as successful in the National League as I was with the Angels in the American League. The biggest adjustment was learning the National League umpires. Back then there were very few options for eating near the old Astrodome. One of the great things about the trend of opening downtown stadiums is that the fans get a wider variety of dining choices—both in and out of the ballpark.

SERVES 8
PREP TIME: 10 MINUTES
COOKING TIME: 12 TO 16 MINUTES

1½ cups light molasses
1 tablespoon whole black peppercorns
½ cup Kentucky bourbon or Tennessee whiskey

½ cup (¼ pound) unsalted butter, chilled and cut into pieces
2 teaspoons fresh lemon juice
8 T-bone steaks, 1 inch thick

¼ cup vegetable oil
2 teaspoons kosher salt
2 teaspoons freshly ground black pepper

---

1 Preheat the grill to medium-high and lightly oil the grill grates.

2 Place the molasses and peppercorns in a medium saucepan and bring to a boil over medium heat. Remove the pan from the heat and whisk in the bourbon, butter, and lemon juice.

3 Transfer 1¼ cups of the sauce to a small saucepan and set over low heat; this will be used for serving. The remainder will be brushed over the steaks while they are on the grill.

4 Brush the steaks with the oil and then season with the salt and pepper.

5 Grill the steaks (in batches, if necessary) for 6 to 8 minutes per side for medium-rare. Baste with the sauce and turn for even cooking. Remove the steaks from the grill and let them rest on a platter for 5 minutes.

6 Serve the steaks with the reserved warm sauce.

Nolan's Serving Tip: My Traditional Green Bean Casserole (page 141) and Loaded Yukon Gold Smashed Potatoes (page 137) are the perfect side dishes for this recipe.

See photograph on page 42.

EASY T-BONE WITH SOY & PINEAPPLE

When I was still pitching for the New York Mets, before I had a regular spot in the starting rotation, Ruth and I would enjoy our time together on those rare opportunities when a weekend day game would allow us to do a cookout for supper. Growing up, we rarely had the time or money to grill steaks, so this was the first time in my life that I could experiment with different cuts of meat to learn what would work best over charcoal.

What I discovered through trial and error was that the T-bone grills consistently and is easy to divide up into smaller portions for your guests who don't want a lot of steak. I still remember these special nights of grilling after Mets games at Shea Stadium, and this set the tone for the cookouts with our young family after I was traded to the Angels and started to make my mark in the game.

SERVES 8
PREP TIME: 5 MINUTES, PLUS 30 MINUTES TO MARINATE THE MEAT
COOKING TIME: 12 TO 16 MINUTES

⅔ cup olive oil
⅓ cup red wine vinegar
¼ cup pineapple juice

¼ cup soy sauce
8 T-bone steaks, 1 inch thick
1 teaspoon kosher salt

1 teaspoon freshly ground black pepper

1 In a large glass baking dish, combine the olive oil, vinegar, pineapple juice, and soy sauce. Set aside ¼ cup of the marinade in a small bowl to use for basting.

2 Add the steaks to the dish and turn to coat well. Set aside at room temperature for 30 minutes.

3 Preheat the grill to medium and lightly oil the grill grates.

4 Drain the steaks and discard the marinade. Season the steaks with salt and pepper and place on the grill. Cook the steaks (in batches, if necessary) for 6 to 8 minutes per side for medium, basting with the reserved marinade and turning the steaks several times. Remove the steaks from the grill and let them rest on a platter for 5 minutes.

GRILLED BBQ T-BONE WITH KENTUCKY BOURBON

T-bones work perfectly on the grill. If I am hosting a big BBQ at my home in Georgetown, or out on the ranch, you can bet that a T-bone will be on the grill, and the reason is consistency.

The first principle of traditional BBQ is that it has to be slow-cooked using only wood smoke for heat. But when you're cooking a steak on an outdoor grill, it's actually the process of direct grilling (cooking the beef directly over the heat) that will intensify the flavors by caramelizing the sugars and proteins at the surface of the steak. A mix of lump charcoal and wood (hickory or mesquite) will make the direct grilling of your T-bones a consistent success. As the fat and liquid from the T-bone drip into the grill, the vapors rise up into the beef to give it a wonderful, smoke-infused flavor.

My very simple combination of Kentucky bourbon and Worcestershire adds another layer of smoke to the beef. I am not a believer in using sauces that distract you from the flavor of the meat. In Cincinnati, the ribs are coated with so much sauce that you never even hear about the ribs—the sauce is the star on the plate, and that's not the Texas way to do BBQ. The sauce or rub should complement the natural flavors, and that's what works so well in my favorite T-bone recipe, which dates back to my playing days with the Houston Astros.

Harry Spilman, a left-handed first baseman with a sweet swing, was one of my best friends on the Astros in the '80s. Harry and I would often go out for dinner on road trips to try T-bone steaks at restaurants all over the country, and we decided that the steaks in Texas always tasted the freshest and had the most flavor.

SERVES 8
PREP TIME: 5 MINUTES, PLUS 10 MINUTES TO MARINATE THE MEAT
COOKING TIME: 10 TO 12 MINUTES

½ cup vegetable oil
½ cup chopped garlic
3 teaspoons Nolan Ryan Steak Seasoning (page 25)

8 T-bone steaks, ¾ to 1 inch thick
⅓ cup Kentucky bourbon
¼ cup Worcestershire sauce

1 to 2 teaspoons kosher salt
1 to 2 teaspoons freshly ground black pepper

---

1 Preheat the grill to medium-high and lightly oil the grill grates.

2 Combine the oil, garlic, and steak seasoning in a large glass baking dish and add the steaks. Turn the steaks to coat well and set aside to marinate for at least 10 minutes.

3 Combine the bourbon and Worcestershire in a small bowl.

4 Drain the steaks, season with salt and pepper, and place on the grill (in batches, if necessary).

Brush the steaks with the bourbon-Worcestershire mixture. Continue to cook the steaks, brushing regularly and turning as needed, until the steaks are caramelized and charred on both sides, 5 to 6 minutes per side for medium.

5 Transfer the steaks to a cutting board and allow to rest for 5 minutes before serving.

Nolan's Serving Tip: Try this with my delicious Potatoes au Gratin (page 134).

GRILLED T-BONE WITH TEQUILA-CHIPOTLE BUTTER SAUCE

I enjoy a margarita on a hot summer day, and tequila has a flavor that I really appreciate in cooking. It's no surprise that Chef Cris would put a Mexican spin on a grilled T-bone steak. For this recipe he came up with an herb butter that has chipotles and banana peppers for spice, which he balances with brown sugar, cilantro, and tequila. The key is placing the chilled butter on the T-bone for no more than 30 seconds so that it melts into the steak while staying around just enough to make the presentation really special.

SERVES 8
PREP TIME: 15 MINUTES, PLUS 1 DAY TO CHILL THE CHILE BUTTER
COOKING TIME: 10 TO 14 MINUTES

1 cup (½ pound) unsalted butter, at room temperature
¼ cup fresh cilantro (leaves only)
1 banana pepper, seeded

2 tablespoons chipotle peppers in adobo sauce
2 tablespoons silver tequila
1 tablespoon brown sugar
1 large yellow onion, cut in half

8 T-bone steaks, 1 inch thick
¼ cup olive oil
2 tablespoons kosher salt
2 tablespoons freshly ground black pepper

1 Place the butter, cilantro, banana pepper, chipotles and adobo, tequila, and brown sugar in a blender or food processor and puree until smooth.

2 Place a sheet of plastic wrap on a work surface. Spoon the chile butter down the center of the plastic wrap. Roll the plastic around the chile butter into a log about 8 inches long. Twist the ends to seal and refrigerate overnight.

3 Preheat the grill to medium-high and lightly oil the grill grates.

4 Using a large fork, rub the grill with the cut sides of the onion halves for a sweet, smoky flavor.

5 Brush the steaks on both sides with the oil and sprinkle with salt and pepper. Grill the steaks (in batches, if necessary) for 5 to 7 minutes per side for medium-rare.

6 Cut the chilled chile butter log crosswise into 8 slices.

7 Place 1 butter slice on each steak, allow the butter to melt into the steaks for 30 seconds, then remove the steaks from the grill and serve.

GRILLED T-BONE WITH SANTA FE PEPPER BUTTER

My son Reid and his wife, Nicole, really enjoy southwestern-style cooking. Reid appreciates how Chef Cris integrates ingredients to create new flavor combinations.

SERVES 8
PREP TIME: 15 MINUTES
COOKING TIME: 14 MINUTES

¾ cup olive oil
¼ cup finely chopped shallots
1 tablespoon chopped garlic
½ cup brandy
1 cup (½ pound) unsalted butter, at room temperature

¼ cup chopped fresh chives
¼ cup Worcestershire sauce
1 tablespoon chili powder
1 teaspoon dry mustard
1 teaspoon paprika

1 teaspoon freshly ground black pepper
1 teaspoon ancho chile powder
8 T-bone steaks, 1¼ inches thick
2 teaspoons kosher salt

1 Heat ½ cup of the oil in a large cast-iron skillet over medium-high heat. Add the shallots, garlic, and brandy and cook, stirring, until the shallots and garlic become soft. Remove the skillet from the heat and set aside to cool.

2 In a small bowl, mix the butter, cooled shallot mixture, chives, Worcestershire, chili powder, mustard, paprika, black pepper, and ancho chile powder until all of the ingredients are combined.

3 Place a sheet of plastic wrap on a work surface. Spoon the chile butter down the center of the plastic wrap. Roll the plastic around the chile butter into a log about 8 inches long. Twist the ends to seal and refrigerate overnight.

4 Preheat the grill to medium-high and lightly oil the grill grates.

5 Brush the steaks with the remaining ¼ cup olive oil and season with the salt.

6 Grill the steaks (in batches, if necessary) for 7 minutes per side for medium-rare. Transfer the steaks to a cutting board to rest for 5 minutes.

7 Remove the butter from the fridge and cut into 16 slices. Place 2 slices of butter on each T-bone and serve.

Nolan's Serving Tip: I like to enjoy this T-bone with freshly sautéed onions.

REID: "Chef Cris is a talented inventor of a type of fusion of Mexican and Texas cooking with exciting new ideas that have transformed the old Tex-Mex—rice, red beans, and chicken or beef cooked with mild spices—into something special. Cris takes fresh-from-the-garden ingredients like serrano peppers, jalapeño peppers, and ancho peppers and works them into dishes that are both innovative and delicious. His Santa Fe pepper butter is a great complement to the T-bone steak."

GRILLED T-BONE WITH RED WINE VINEGAR & CAPER-GARLIC SAUCE

In this recipe, we use butter to soften the strong flavors of red wine vinegar, capers, and garlic. Each bite gives you a punch of flavor from the sauce without obscuring the purity of the T-bone.

SERVES 8
PREP TIME: 10 MINUTES
COOKING TIME 10 TO 14 MINUTES

¼ bunch curly parsley, chopped (leaves only)

¼ cup capers

1 garlic clove, minced

2 tablespoons red wine vinegar

1 tablespoon freshly ground black pepper, plus more for seasoning the steaks

1½ teaspoons kosher salt, plus more for seasoning the steaks

¼ cup unsalted butter, melted

¼ cup olive oil

8 T-bone steaks, 1¼ inches thick

1 Preheat the grill to high and lightly oil the grill grates.

2 In a medium bowl, mix the parsley, capers, garlic, vinegar, pepper, and salt.

3 Whisk the melted butter, in increments, into the sauce.

4 Brush the steaks on both sides with the oil and season with salt and pepper. Grill the steaks (in batches, if necessary) for 5 to 7 minutes per side for medium, brushing continually with the sauce. Transfer the steaks to a cutting board to rest for 5 minutes.

5 Serve the steaks with the reserved sauce.

GRILLED TEXAS STRIP STEAK

This strip steak recipe is one of my favorites. Simply marinated in garlic, oil, beef base, and bourbon, the beef takes on an incredible flavor. You can find strip steaks cut to different thicknesses, and this will determine how long they take to cook on a grill. A 1½-inch-thick strip steak will take approximately 12 minutes for medium-rare and up to 18 minutes for medium-well.

SERVES 8
PREP TIME: 5 MINUTES, PLUS 1 HOUR TO MARINATE THE MEAT
COOKING TIME: 12 TO 18 MINUTES

4½ cups vegetable oil
¼ cup bourbon
2 tablespoons beef base

3 garlic cloves, minced
8 (10- to 12-ounce) New York strip steaks, 1½ inches thick

2 teaspoons kosher salt
2 teaspoons pepper

Nolan's Tip: Beef base, a concentrated liquid stock, adds depth of flavor to all of your steaks.

1 In a large glass baking dish, combine the oil, bourbon, beef base, and garlic. Set aside ¼ cup of the marinade in a small bowl to use for basting.

2 Add the steaks to the dish and turn to coat well. Let the steaks marinate at room temperature for 1 hour.

3 Preheat the grill to high and lightly oil the grill grates.

4 Drain the steaks and discard the marinade. Pat with a paper towel to absorb excess oil and season with salt and pepper. Cook the steaks (in batches, if necessary) for 5 to 7 minutes per side for medium-rare, basting continually with the reserved marinade.

5 Transfer the steaks to a cutting board and let the meat rest for 5 minutes before serving.

3

TENDERLOIN & SIRLOIN

CHILLED ROASTED BEEF TENDERLOIN WITH CREAM OF HORSERADISH

Once I started my ranch business and became heavily involved with producing beef cattle, it was only a matter of time before I'd tried just about every variation on tenderloin, and I can tell you that I have yet to find a bad tenderloin dish. This take on a classic Texas dish is served chilled with a side of cream of horseradish. I'm not one to use horseradish on any meat dish unless it's made by Chef Cris in this excellent recipe.

I met a sports agent for dinner recently at Del Frisco's in Fort Worth, and he put so much horseradish on his steak that there was no way in the world he could taste anything but the horseradish. I'm a believer in showcasing the flavor of the beef, and tenderloin is one of the bolder cuts, so I suggest going relatively light on the sauce.

SERVES 10 TO 12
PREP TIME: 5 MINUTES, PLUS 1 DAY TO CHILL THE MEAT
COOKING TIME: 20 TO 25 MINUTES

⅓ cup Dijon mustard
⅓ cup Worcestershire sauce
2 tablespoons chopped garlic

1 (4- to 5-pound) beef tenderloin, cleaned and trimmed
¼ cup Nolan Ryan Steak Seasoning (page 25)

1 teaspoon kosher salt
1 teaspoon freshly ground black pepper
1 recipe Cream of Horseradish (recipe follows)

Nolan's Tip: If your tenderloin is not trimmed in advance by the butcher, use a sharp knife to remove the chain—the rope of connective tissue—and all excess fat, without removing any of the usable meat.

1 Preheat the oven to 350°F.

2 In a small bowl, combine the mustard, Worcestershire sauce, and garlic. Place the tenderloin on a baking sheet and spread the sauce evenly over all surfaces of the meat. Season with the steak seasoning, salt, and pepper.

3 Bake the tenderloin until the internal temperature reaches 110°F to 115°F for medium-rare, 20 to 25 minutes.

4 Remove the beef from the oven and turn it upside-down on the baking sheet; this will allow the juices to flow back in. Cover and chill overnight.

5 When ready to serve, slice thin and dress lightly with the horseradish sauce.

Cream of Horseradish

Makes about 1 cup
Prep time: 5 minutes

1 cup sour cream
3 teaspoons prepared horseradish
1 teaspoon Worcestershire sauce
Dash of cayenne pepper

Combine all of the ingredients and stir well. Cover and chill for at least 1 hour to allow the flavors to meld.

WILD MUSHROOM & CRANBERRY—STUFFED TENDERLOIN WITH PORT WINE PAN SAUCE

We don't have wild mushrooms here in Texas, but some people seek out exotic varieties to add a nutty, earthy flavor to their dishes. Bright orange sulfur shelf mushrooms, also known as chicken mushrooms, grow throughout North America (but not in Texas), Africa, and Europe and have a mild, sweet flavor. If you can't find chicken mushrooms, shiitake or portobello mushrooms will work just fine in this recipe.

You can use dried or fresh cranberries for the mushroom mixture, but fresh berries give more of a kick of flavor. I look at this recipe as a seasonal specialty of autumn, when cranberries are in season. But dried cranberries are available year-round, so feel free to give this a try whenever you are in the mood for something special.

SERVES 10 TO 12
PREP TIME: 10 MINUTES
COOKING TIME: 30 TO 45 MINUTES

---

1 (4- to 5-pound) tenderloin, cleaned and trimmed
1 recipe Wild Mushrooms and Cranberries (recipe follows)

3 tablespoons Nolan Ryan Steak Seasoning (page 25)
2 tablespoons ground coriander

3 tablespoons vegetable oil
1 recipe Port Wine Pan Sauce (recipe follows)

---

1 Preheat the oven to 350°F.

2 Butterfly the tenderloin and pound to an even ½-inch thickness.

3 Spread an even layer of the mushroom-cranberry mixture across the entire surface of the tenderloin. Tightly roll the tenderloin and tie with butcher's twine.

4 Combine the steak seasoning and coriander; evenly coat the tenderloin on all sides with this spice mixture.

5 In a large roasting pan, heat the oil over high heat until it's almost smoking. Sear all sides of the tenderloin.

6 Place the tenderloin on a roasting rack in the roasting pan and roast until the internal temperature reaches 155°F on a meat thermometer, 30 to 45 minutes. Let it rest for 10 minutes, then cut into ½-inch slices. Serve with the warm port wine pan sauce.

Wild Mushrooms & Cranberries

Makes about 3 cups
Prep time: 15 minutes

¼ cup vegetable oil

1 tablespoon chopped garlic

2 chicken mushrooms or 2 portobello mushroom caps, diced

2 oyster mushrooms, sliced

1 tablespoon kosher salt

2 cups dry red wine

1 cup panko bread crumbs

2 poblano peppers, seeded and diced small

2 cups fresh or dried cranberries, coarsely chopped

1 Heat the oil in a large saucepan; add the garlic and sauté until light brown, about 30 seconds.

2 Add the mushrooms and salt and sauté until the mushrooms are tender, 3 to 5 minutes.

3 Add the red wine and simmer until the pan is almost dry. Remove the pan from the heat and let cool. Pour the cooled mixture into a food processor and pulse until fine. Transfer the mixture to a medium bowl, and stir in the bread crumbs, poblano peppers, and cranberries.

Port Wine Pan Sauce

Makes about 4 cups
Prep time: 30 minutes

2½ tablespoons unsalted butter

2 shallots, chopped fine

2 tablespoons chopped fresh thyme

1 garlic clove, minced

2 cups port

2 cups beef broth

1 Melt the butter in a medium skillet over medium heat. Add the shallots, thyme, and garlic. Cook, stirring constantly, until the shallots become tender and soft.

2 Add the port and start scraping up any shallot bits from the bottom of the pan.

3 Bring the port to a boil, reduce the heat to medium, and let the liquid reduce by half. Stir in the beef broth and cook for 15 minutes.

4 Remove the skillet from the heat and cover to keep warm until ready to serve.

Nolan's Serving Tip: Loaded Yukon Gold Smashed Potatoes (page 137) are the perfect side dish for this tenderloin.

CLASSIC CHATEAUBRIAND

Chateaubriand is one of the more sophisticated offerings among my favorites. But first let's put aside the confusion over the name, which does not refer to the cut of the meat but rather to the recipe itself. Chateaubriand is made from a thick cut from the center section of the tenderloin—the portion of the tenderloin contained in the porterhouse section of the beef loin.

SERVES 6 TO 8
PREP TIME: 5 MINUTES, PLUS 30 MINUTES TO MARINATE THE MEAT
COOKING TIME: 36 MINUTES

For the marinade:
¼ white onion, finely chopped
2 tablespoons beef base
2 tablespoons olive oil
1 tablespoon chopped garlic

1 tablespoon kosher salt
1 tablespoon freshly ground black pepper

1 (4- to 5-pound) beef tenderloin, cleaned and trimmed

For seasoning on the cutting board:
¼ cup olive oil
1 teaspoon sea salt
1 teaspoon freshly ground black pepper

Nolan's Tip: Don't ask your butcher for a Chateaubriand; the right cut to ask for is the "whole head filet" or "stub tender." Almost all beef sirloins are boned out these days, so there are plenty of head filets available.

1 In a small bowl, combine all of the marinade ingredients. Put the meat on a large platter and rub the marinade into the meat with your hands. Allow the meat to marinate for 30 minutes at room temperature.

2 Preheat the oven to 375°F and the grill to medium. Lightly oil the grill grates.

3 Grill the tenderloin for 8 minutes; turn and cook for another 8 minutes. Transfer the tenderloin to a large roasting pan and finish in the oven until the internal temperature reaches 110°F to 115°F for medium-rare, about 20 minutes.

4 Transfer the meat to a cutting board and let it rest for 10 minutes.

5 In a small bowl, combine the olive oil, salt, and pepper and pour the mixture over the meat on the cutting board. Slice the meat, turning to coat it evenly with the dressing.

PROSCIUTTO-WRAPPED BEEF TENDERLOIN IN BURGUNDY SAUCE OVER GNOCCHI

This is one of the most creative applications of tenderloin that I have ever had the pleasure to taste. The prosciutto adds a salty element, while the Burgundy adds enough balance to ensure that the flavor of the tenderloin still shines through. Tenderloin is extremely versatile, and this is another example of how Chef Cris weaves complementary flavors together in unexpected ways.

SERVES 8
PREP TIME: 20 MINUTES
COOKING TIME: 20 TO 30 MINUTES

8 (6-ounce) beef tenderloin steaks
6 tablespoons olive oil
1 teaspoon kosher salt
1 teaspoon freshly ground black pepper
8 fresh sage leaves
8 thin slices prosciutto
2 cups red Burgundy wine
4 cups beef broth
6 tablespoons unsalted butter, chilled and cut into pieces
1 pound fresh, frozen, or dried gnocchi

1 Preheat the oven to 350°F.

2 Rub the tenderloins with the olive oil and season with the salt and pepper.

3 Place one sage leaf on each tenderloin and wrap with prosciutto; secure with a wooden skewer.

4 Heat a large sauté pan on high heat and sear the tenderloins (in batches, if necessary) for 2 minutes per side. Remove from the heat and place in an oven-safe roasting pan.

5 Place the pan in the oven and bake for 10 to 15 minutes.

6 Meanwhile, pour the wine into the same pan used for searing the tenderloins. Bring the wine to a boil and cook until reduced by half, and then turn the heat down to a simmer.

7 In a medium saucepan, bring the broth to a boil, add the reduced wine, and simmer for 5 minutes. Remove the pot from the heat and whisk in the butter.

8 Bring a large pot of salted water to a boil. Cook the gnocchi until al dente, following the package directions.

9 Drain the gnocchi and transfer to a platter or shallow serving bowl. Pour the wine sauce over the gnocchi and top with the tenderloins.

Nolan's Serving Tip: I like to serve my Spinach Casserole (page 142) on the side to add some color to the plate.

BEEF TENDERLOIN & BLACK BEAN QUESADILLA

The thing that sets Chef Cris's recipes apart is that they have bold southwestern flavors but not too much spice. In this recipe, the pepper jack cheese and black beans add a great balance for the tenderloin, cilantro, and jalapeño peppers. This recipe also draws out the savory, smoky flavors of the tenderloin with the toasty, tart flavors of the peppers and green onions. Chef Cris has put together a crowd pleaser, and that's what cooking is all about—making people happy.

SERVES 10
PREP TIME: 30 MINUTES
COOKING TIME: 5 MINUTES

2 (15-ounce) cans black beans, rinsed and drained
½ cup finely chopped scallions
¼ cup chopped fresh cilantro
2 jalapeño peppers, seeded and chopped

1½ teaspoons chopped garlic
1 teaspoon kosher salt
1 teaspoon freshly ground black pepper
¼ cup vegetable oil, plus more for brushing the tortillas

2 pounds beef tenderloin tips
10 large flour tortillas
2 pounds pepper jack cheese, shredded

1 Place the beans, scallions, cilantro, jalapeños, garlic, salt, and pepper in a large saucepan over medium heat. Cook the beans for 15 minutes. Pour the mixture through a sieve into the sink to drain off all the liquid. Transfer the solids to a blender or food processor and puree until smooth.

2 Heat the oil in a large skillet over high heat. Pan-sear the beef tips (in batches, if necessary), turning frequently, about 5 minutes for medium-rare. Transfer the meat to a cutting board and let it rest for 5 minutes to retain its juices, and then slice thin.

3 To assemble the quesadillas, spread some of the black bean mixture on each flour tortilla. Sprinkle some cheese evenly over the top. Place some sliced beef on half of the tortilla. Fold the tortilla in half and brush with oil on both sides.

4 Heat another large skillet over medium heat and pan-sear the quesadillas until golden brown on both sides, a minute or two.

5 Remove the quesadillas from the heat, cut each into 6 wedges, and serve.

MINI CHICKEN-FRIED BEEF TENDERLOIN STEAK SANDWICHES WITH JALAPEÑO COUNTRY GRAVY

Texans are picky about their chicken-fried steak with gravy, and I'm no different. My first experience with country gravy was when my mom made biscuits with sausage gravy, and this still stands out as one of the best things I ever ate. I was in the U.S. Army for six months of active duty and then in the reserves for five and a half years, and I was served biscuits and gravy every day at breakfast.

My commitment to the U.S. Army ended when I was traded to the Angels. Given the opportunity to start every fourth day, I could finally prove that I could make an impact as a power pitcher. The Angels, who were in a rebuilding mode, let me work out some of the problems with my delivery.

This versatile recipe is a play on country gravy and chicken-fried steak, but it turns it into a fun and bold-flavored steak sandwich that's got the Southwest flavor of jalapeño and just the right amount of onion and garlic. I believe in versatility in all things in life.

SERVES 8 TO 10
PREP TIME: 20 MINUTES
COOKING TIME: 5 MINUTES

For the steaks:
1½ cups vegetable oil
1 (2-pound) beef tenderloin, cut into 18 pieces
1½ cups all-purpose flour
2 teaspoons kosher salt
1 teaspoon freshly ground black pepper

¼ teaspoon garlic powder
¼ teaspoon onion powder
2 large eggs
1¼ cups whole milk

For the gravy:
¼ cup finely chopped jalapeño peppers

¼ cup all-purpose flour
1 teaspoon kosher salt
1 teaspoon freshly ground black pepper
2 cups whole milk

18 country biscuits

1 Heat a large cast-iron skillet over high heat for approximately 7 minutes, then add the vegetable oil and allow it to get hot.

2 Meanwhile, pound each steak piece between two sheets of wax paper or plastic wrap until very thin, using a heavy weight or the side of a cleaver.

3 In a shallow dish, combine the flour, salt, pepper, garlic powder, and onion powder and mix well.

4 In a medium bowl, combine the eggs and the milk.

5 Place the steaks, two at a time, in the seasoned flour mixture. Dip the floured steaks in the dish with the egg-milk mixture, and then dredge them again in the flour mixture. Place the batter-coated steaks on a baking sheet lined with wax paper.

6 Sauté the meat (in batches, if necessary) until golden brown on both sides, about a minute. Transfer the steaks to a platter as they are done.

7 When all of the steaks are cooked, make the gravy. Pour ⅓ cup of the pan drippings into a small saucepan set over medium heat. Add the jalapeño peppers, flour, salt, and pepper and whisk until completely blended.

8 Add the milk and continue to stir until the mixture thickens to the texture of classic country gravy.

9 Open each biscuit and add a mini chicken-fried steak. Serve the gravy on the side.

Nolan's Serving Tip: I like to serve the gravy on the side so that the bread does not fall apart.

GRILLED FILET MIGNON WITH CHILES & HERBS

Filet mignon is my standard choice when I go out to eat with Ruth at Del Frisco's in Fort Worth. I devised this recipe to be somewhat more advanced than many others, but the time and effort are well worth it. The filet mignon is rich with flavor from the marriage of the marinade with the smoke and coals from the outdoor grill.

SERVES 8
PREP TIME: 10 MINUTES, PLUS 3 HOURS TO MARINATE THE MEAT
COOKING TIME: 12 MINUTES

For the marinade:
1 cup olive oil
2 tablespoons red wine vinegar
1 tablespoon freshly ground black pepper
2 thyme sprigs
1 rosemary sprig

8 (6-ounce) filet mignon steaks

For the relish:
¼ cup olive oil
3 tablespoons unsalted butter, melted
1 tablespoon olive oil
¼ cup finely chopped red onion
4 garlic cloves, minced
1 tablespoon chopped fresh parsley

1 tablespoon diced green chiles, seeded
1 teaspoon grated lemon zest

For the filets:
1 to 2 teaspoons sea salt
1 to 2 teaspoons freshly ground black pepper
1 to 2 tablespoons vegetable oil

1 Combine all of the marinade ingredients in a glass baking dish and mix well. Add the steaks and turn to coat. Cover and marinate in the refrigerator for 3 hours.

2 For the relish, combine all of the ingredients in a small bowl and mix thoroughly. Place half of the relish in a separate small bowl and set alongside the grill.

3 Preheat the grill to medium-high and lightly oil the grill grates.

4 Remove the steaks from the marinade, pat dry with heavy-duty paper towels, and season with salt and pepper. Drizzle with the vegetable oil.

5 Cook the steaks (in batches, if necessary) for 6 minutes per side for medium-rare. Baste with some of the relish mixture while cooking to ensure that the meat is beautifully caramelized.

6 Turn the steaks over and place them on a serving platter. Top with the remaining relish and serve.

BLACKENED BEEF WITH GRILLED CORN, JALAPEÑO & BELL PEPPER SAUCE

This simple southwestern dish packs a whole lot of intense flavor. By cooking the corn on the grill, letting it brown and blister, you bring out the burnt sugar from the corn. The jalapeño and bell pepper sauce packs even more flavor, but not so much as to disguise the essence of the meat. My son Reid and his wife, Nicole, really enjoy this recipe.

SERVES 8
PREP TIME: 45 MINUTES
COOKING TIME: 8 MINUTES

---

5 ears of corn, with husks
4 teaspoons olive oil
1 large white onion, diced
¼ cup tomato paste
1¼ cups red wine
3 cups beef broth
1 thyme sprig

1 teaspoon kosher salt
1 tablespoon unsalted butter
1 large red bell pepper, seeded and diced
1 large green bell pepper, seeded and diced
2 teaspoons diced seeded jalapeño pepper

4 garlic cloves, chopped
2 to 3 shallots, chopped fine
1 teaspoon chopped fresh cilantro
1 teaspoon Worcestershire sauce
1 teaspoon hot sauce
8 (4- to 5-ounce) beef tenderloin steaks
½ cup Cajun Seasoning (page 25)

---

1 Preheat the oven to 375°F and the grill to medium-high. Lightly oil the grill grates.

2 Soak the corn in cold water for 5 minutes to moisten the husks. Place the corn in a roasting pan and roast for 15 minutes.

3 Remove the husks and silk and place the corn on the grill. Cook until golden brown on all sides.

4 With a sharp knife, slice the kernels off the cob into a medium bowl. Reserve the cobs for the sauce.

5 Heat 2 teaspoons of the olive oil in a deep sauté pan over medium-high heat. When the oil begins to shimmer, add the onion and sauté until brown. Stir in the tomato paste, and then add the wine and reduce until almost dry.

6 Add the broth, corncobs, thyme, and salt. Simmer until the sauce reduces by one-quarter. Remove the corncobs and strain the sauce through a fine-mesh sieve into a small bowl and reserve.

7 Return the pan to medium heat and melt the butter. Add the corn kernels, bell peppers, jalapeño pepper, garlic, shallots, and cilantro. Sauté until the peppers are tender.

8 Add the Worcestershire sauce, hot sauce, and reserved strained sauce to the pan, reduce the heat to low, and simmer for 8 minutes.

9 Season the tenderloins with Cajun Seasoning on both sides.

10 Heat the remaining 2 teaspoons olive oil in a large cast-iron skillet and sauté the tenderloins (in batches, if necessary) for 4 minutes per side for medium-rare.

11 Serve the tenderloins with the warm sauce and enjoy.

REID: "I enjoy the way Chef Cris can use jalapeño peppers to bring something fresh and creative to a beautiful cut of tenderloin."

TEXAS TENDERLOIN TIPS IN RED WINE MUSHROOM SAUCE

Most chefs pride themselves on a perfectly cooked tenderloin. The meat has to be moist and flavorful, and the preparation has to go well with the rich flavors of the beef. After trying many different cooking methods, Chef Cris has hit upon several very fine recipes. In this careful strategy to cooking tenderloin to bring out its best, we cook the beef in a sauté pan (rather than grilling) and whip up a sauce that includes red wine, heavy cream, and a rich beef broth, which adds a lot of depth to the dish.

SERVES 8 TO 10
PREP TIME: 25 MINUTES
COOKING TIME: 10 TO 13 MINUTES

- ½ cup (8 tablespoons) vegetable oil
- 1 large yellow onion, diced
- 4 medium carrots, peeled and cut into ½-inch pieces
- 1 celery rib, cut into ½-inch pieces
- 8 ounces white mushroom caps, cut in half

- 4 pounds beef tenderloin tips, cut into 1-inch chunks
- 1 teaspoon kosher salt
- 1 teaspoon freshly ground black pepper
- ½ cup (¼ pound) unsalted butter

- ½ cup all-purpose flour
- 1 cup dry red wine
- 2 cups beef broth
- 1 cup sour cream
- ½ cup heavy cream

---

1 Heat 5 tablespoons of the oil in a deep sauté pan over medium heat. Cook the onion for 1 minute, add the carrots and cook for 1 minute, add the celery and cook for 1 minute, and then add the mushrooms and cook for 2 minutes. Make sure all of the vegetables are tender. Transfer the vegetables to a plate.

2 Add the remaining 3 tablespoons vegetable oil to the still-hot sauté pan and add the beef (in batches, if necessary). Season with the salt and pepper. Cook, turning often, for 8 to 10 minutes for medium.

3 Stir in the butter until melted. Dust the meat with the flour, and cook until the beef is golden brown, 2 to 3 minutes.

4 Transfer the beef to a plate and tent with foil to keep warm.

5 Deglaze the pan with the red wine, stir, and cook until reduced by half.

6 Add the beef broth, sour cream, and heavy cream. Cook for 8 minutes, stirring constantly, and then reduce the heat to low and simmer for 10 minutes.

7 Serve the beef with the warm sauce.

Nolan's Serving Tip: Serve the tenderloin tips with a generous portion of Green Bean Casserole (page 141).

TENDERLOIN MEDALLIONS WITH TOMATO-OLIVE RAGOUT

I will admit that I am not a big fan of olives. Putting them in a sauce for tenderloin was a leap of faith for me. But Charlie Bradbury, CEO of Nolan Ryan Beef, loves olives, so this one is for him.

SERVES 8
PREP TIME: 15 TO 20 MINUTES
COOKING TIME: 4 TO 6 MINUTES

2 tablespoons clarified butter (see Tip below)
20 green olives, pitted and chopped
1 tablespoon chopped garlic
8 plum tomatoes, peeled, diced, and seeded

1½ cups beef broth
½ cup dry red wine
2 teaspoons chopped fresh tarragon
2 teaspoons chopped fresh basil
2 teaspoons kosher salt

2 teaspoons freshly ground black pepper
8 (4-ounce) beef tenderloin steaks
¼ cup olive oil

1 Preheat the grill to medium-high and lightly oil the grill grates.

2 Melt the clarified butter in a medium sauté pan over medium heat. Add the olives, garlic, and diced tomatoes.

3 Sauté for 1 minute, stirring, and then add the beef broth, wine, tarragon, basil, and 1 teaspoon each of the salt and pepper. Turn the heat to low and simmer for 5 minutes. Transfer the sauce to a bowl and set aside.

4 Brush the steaks with the olive oil and season with the remaining 1 teaspoon each salt and pepper.

5 Grill the steaks (in batches, if necessary) for 2 to 3 minutes per side for medium-rare. Transfer to a cutting board to rest for 5 minutes.

6 Serve the tenderloins with the sauce.

Nolan's Technique Tip: Clarified butter has a higher smoke point than regular butter. It can be made in advance and refrigerated or frozen. Place ½ cup (¼ pound) butter in a heavy-bottomed saucepan over low heat. Cook until it is completely melted, about 2 minutes. Remove from the heat and cool until the butter separates, about 5 minutes. Skim the foam off the top and carefully pour the clear, yellow butter into a clean container. Discard the milk solids at the bottom of the pan.

TEXAS SURF & TURF PLATTER WITH FIERY TENDERLOIN, JUMBO SHRIMP & CILANTRO RÉMOULADE

This recipe depends on hot sauce and Cajun seasoning for just the right punch of flavor. I'm fine with spicy food, but not to the point where it numbs your taste buds. I've seen people eat so many chile "patines" (native to Texas) that they can't taste anything else—that's a waste of good eating.

When I pitched for the Texas Rangers, the original "ballpark nacho" was introduced at Arlington Stadium—all you got was a big tortilla chip with jalapeño peppers and cheese sauce on top. I could never see the attraction to that item, but it's possible that people completely lose their sense of taste after eating a certain number of jalapeños.

SERVES 6
PREP TIME: 30 MINUTES
COOKING TIME: 10 MINUTES

For the shrimp:
6 slices smoked bacon
½ cup fine bread crumbs
6 ounces Boursin cheese
6 jumbo shrimp (ask the fishmonger for U10 or U12)
1 teaspoon kosher salt
1 teaspoon freshly ground black pepper
⅓ cup dry white wine

For the tenderloins:
½ cup olive oil
6 (4-ounce) beef tenderloin steaks
3 tablespoons Cajun Seasoning (page 25)
1 teaspoon kosher salt
1 teaspoon freshly ground black pepper
1 cup Kentucky bourbon or Tennessee whiskey

1 tablespoon Worcestershire sauce
1 tablespoon hot sauce
½ cup (¼ pound) unsalted butter, at room temperature
1 recipe Cilantro Rémoulade (page 29)

1 Preheat the oven to 325°F.

2 Place the bacon on a baking sheet and cook until partially done, 8 to 10 minutes. Transfer the bacon to a plate lined with paper towels and pat dry.

3 Combine the bread crumbs and Boursin and divide into six equal portions.

4 Peel and devein the shrimp, but leave the tails on (see Tip below). Butterfly the shrimp, cutting from the back and leaving the tails intact.

5 Stuff the cheese mixture inside the shrimp, wrap with bacon, and secure with a wooden skewer. Place the shrimp on a baking sheet coated with nonstick olive oil spray. Season the shrimp with salt and pepper and a splash of white wine.

6 Bake the shrimp until the bacon is perfectly cooked, 12 to 15 minutes. Transfer the shrimp to a platter and tent with foil to keep warm.

7 While the shrimp is baking, cook the tenderloins. Pour the oil into a large cast-iron skillet and heat over high heat until it begins to smoke. Season the steaks on both sides with the Cajun seasoning, salt, and pepper.

8 Cook the steaks (in batches, if necessary) in the skillet for 5 minutes per side for medium-rare. Transfer the steaks to a large platter.

9 Reduce the heat to low and add the bourbon, Worcestershire, and hot sauce. Stir in the butter and remove from the heat.

10 Pour the warm sauce over the steaks. Place one shrimp on top of each steak and serve with cilantro rémoulade on the side.

Nolan's Technique Tip: The "vein" of the shrimp is its digestive tract, and in most cases it is preferable to devein because of the common perception that a shrimp with veins is gritty to the tongue. In this recipe, Chef Cris leaves the tails on, so the choice of deveining or not comes down to personal preference. Many fishmongers will do it for you. However, if you are doing it yourself, the technique is basic: Grasp a shrimp between thumb and forefinger, one-third of an inch behind where the head is cut off. Position the tip of a paring knife (blade facing up) into the indentation near the top of the body of the shrimp and push with pressure toward the tail. This will make a slight incision the length of the back of the shrimp, which in turn exposes the vein. Remove it with the tip of the paring knife.

SOUTHERN BEEF WELLINGTON WITH RED WINE SAUCE

I enjoy drinking wine with a good meal, red wine in particular, because it brings out the natural flavors of the ingredients. This take on a traditional beef Wellington—a tenderloin wrapped in puff pastry and filled with a savory blend of cheese and bacon—is elevated to another level by a sauce made with beef broth, butter, and good red table wine. It is a fine way to change things up with tenderloin, a different spin on cooking steak.

SERVES 8
PREP TIME: 35 MINUTES
COOKING TIME: 17 TO 21 MINUTES

For the beef Wellington:
8 ounces bacon
8 (4-ounce) beef tenderloin steaks
1 teaspoon kosher salt
1 teaspoon freshly ground black pepper
8 ounces sharp cheddar cheese, shredded
¼ bunch cilantro, chopped (leaves only)
¼ bunch scallions, chopped fine
8 (4- by 5-inch) sheets fresh or frozen puff pastry (you may need to trim the larger store-bought pastry sheets), at room temperature
2 large eggs
¼ cup water

For the red wine sauce:
1 cup dry red wine
1 cup beef broth
2 tablespoons unsalted butter
1 teaspoon kosher salt
1 teaspoon freshly ground black pepper

1 Preheat the oven to 400°F.

2 Cook the bacon in a large skillet over medium-high heat until crisp. Drain off the fat and pat the bacon dry with paper towels. Chop the bacon and set aside.

3 Increase the heat to high. Season the tenderloins with salt and pepper. Sear the tenderloins for 2 minutes on each side. Transfer the steaks to a plate and place in the fridge for 10 minutes. Keep the seasoned skillet on hand for the red wine sauce.

4 In a small bowl, combine the cheese, chopped bacon, cilantro, and scallions.

5 Lay the puff pastry sheets out on your work surface. Spoon some of the cheese-bacon mixture onto the center of each puff pastry; place a tenderloin on top of each. Wrap the puff pastry around the beef and place on an oiled baking sheet.

6 Whisk together the eggs and water; brush this egg wash over the tops of the puff pastry packets.

7 Bake until the puff pastry turns golden brown, 13 to 17 minutes.

8 Meanwhile, prepare the red wine sauce. Reheat the skillet over medium heat. Add the wine and cook until it has reduced by half.

9 Add the beef broth, bring to a boil, and then turn the heat down and let it simmer until it again reduces by half.

10 Add the butter and let it cook into the sauce. Season with salt and pepper.

11 Serve the beef Wellingtons with the warm sauce.

BBQ SIRLOIN SKEWERS WRAPPED IN BACON

Sirloin has a bolder flavor than any other cut of beef. It is not as tender as many other cuts, though, and that's why I rarely order it in a restaurant. My favorite steak dish in restaurants is a filet mignon, followed by a boneless rib-eye steak and then a T-bone, provided it's been cooked on a grill. I never order a porterhouse because it is too big. I don't want to order a steak for two or three people and try to figure out how to make sure everyone has a piece of meat that's cooked perfectly.

Chef Cris has solved the problem of tenderizing sirloin by cutting it into cubes and adding moisture and flavor through a combination of barbecue sauce, steak sauce, and Worcestershire sauce. The secret to success with sirloin is grilling the meat until it is almost done and then taking it the rest of the way to medium-rare in the oven for 5 minutes.

SERVES 8
PREP TIME: 5 MINUTES
COOKING TIME: 15 MINUTES

¼ cup Worcestershire sauce

2 tablespoons steak sauce of your choice

2 pounds boneless top sirloin, cut into ¾-inch-thick strips

1 teaspoon Nolan Ryan Steak Seasoning (page 25)

1 teaspoon kosher salt

1 teaspoon freshly ground black pepper

16 slices thick-cut bacon

1 cup barbecue sauce of your choice

Nolan's Grilling Tip: The grill must be a well-oiled surface for cooking. To apply oil to the grill, use a folded kitchen towel.

1 Preheat the grill to high and the oven to 375°F. Lightly oil the grill grates. Soak 16 wooden skewers in water for at least 10 minutes.

2 Combine the Worcestershire sauce and steak sauce in a glass baking dish. Toss the beef in the sauce and add the steak seasoning, salt, and pepper.

3 Thread the beef cubes onto the skewers and wrap the beef with the bacon.

4 Place the skewers on the grill (in batches, if necessary) and cook for 10 minutes, turning constantly, until the bacon is cooked three-quarters of the way to crisp.

5 Transfer the skewers to a baking sheet. Brush with the barbecue sauce and finish cooking in the oven for 5 minutes.

GRILLED SIRLOIN KABOBS

What makes this recipe so flavorful is the southwestern marinade of chipotle peppers packed in adobo sauce, oil and vinegar dressing, garlic, and Worcestershire. The key step in the recipe is allowing the beef cubes to marinate for at least 3 hours to absorb the piquant flavors of the peppers and the acidic notes of the vinegar and tangy garlic.

SERVES 8
PREP TIME: 15 MINUTES, PLUS 3 HOURS TO MARINATE THE MEAT
COOKING TIME: 10 TO 15 MINUTES

⅔ cup olive oil
⅓ cup distilled white vinegar
¼ cup Worcestershire sauce
1 tablespoon chipotle peppers in adobo sauce

1 teaspoon chopped garlic
2 pounds boneless top sirloin, cut into 1½-inch cubes
1 teaspoon kosher salt
1 teaspoon freshly ground black pepper

3 large bell peppers, cut into 1-inch dice
8 large mushrooms, halved
1 large yellow onion, quartered and separated into pieces

Nolan's Grilling Tip: The fat and moisture from the sirloin kabobs that drop down into the charcoal actually vaporize and rise back up to the meat, adding another layer of intense flavor. With sirloin, a cut that tends to dry out quickly, apply oil or baste with the marinade to prevent the crust of the sirloin from drying out.

1 Prepare the marinade by combining the olive oil, vinegar, Worcestershire, chipotle peppers and adobo sauce, and garlic in a large glass baking dish. Mix well. Set aside ¼ cup of the marinade in a small bowl, cover, and place in the fridge to use later for basting.

2 Coat the beef cubes in the marinade, cover the dish, and place in the fridge to marinate for 3 hours.

3 Preheat the grill to high and lightly oil the grill grates. Soak 16 wooden skewers in water for at least 10 minutes.

4 Drain the beef and discard the marinade. Season the beef with salt and pepper. Set up your kabobs by threading beef cubes on the skewers and alternating with bell peppers, mushrooms, and onions.

5 Grill the kabobs (in batches, if necessary) until cooked to medium-rare, turning and basting frequently with the reserved marinade, 10 to 15 minutes.

4

ROASTS
& SUNDAY SPECIALS

SLOW-ROASTED PRIME RIB WITH NATURAL JUS

I never ate prime rib in my life until I signed with the New York Mets and started going out to restaurants with the veteran players on the team. The idea of "going out to dinner" was a whole new experience for me, and I loved the opportunity to try new foods, flavors, and dishes that were not on my radar while growing up in Texas.

My mom was a very good cook and we had some great down-home comfort meals, like fried chicken with country gravy. Some of my favorites that my mom prepared were liver and onions (I still enjoy eating calf's liver) and Sunday pot roast. I looked forward to those special Sunday dinners all week long. I dreamed of eating fried chicken while I was playing baseball or basketball down the street from our home in Alvin. But we never ate prime rib at home—and even steak was a rarity because it was considered a luxury. Growing up in a rural town meant we ate all our meals at home, and prime rib was considered restaurant food.

This recipe reminds me of the great prime rib I discovered at Lawry's Prime Rib in Chicago, where you pick your cut right off the rolling cart and it is sliced tableside. This version has a rich, complex flavor and the textbook caramelized crust, but the genius of the recipe lies in the way it manages to retain the moist and tender quality of the beef.

Chef Cris shows you how to make great *jus* from the drippings. But all you purists, like me, can just add salt and pepper to enjoy the natural flavor of this perfect prime rib.

SERVES 8 TO 10
PREP TIME: 30 MINUTES
COOKING TIME: 3 HOURS

For the prime rib:
½ cup Dijon mustard
¼ cup Worcestershire sauce
2 tablespoons chopped garlic
½ of a boneless prime rib (An average prime rib weighs 14 to 16 pounds; buy a whole prime rib if cooking for a large crowd and double the recipe.)
½ cup Nolan Ryan Steak Seasoning (page 25)

For the *jus*:
¼ cup vegetable oil
2 celery ribs, cut into chunks
1 medium carrot, peeled and cut into chunks
1 medium yellow onion, peeled and quartered
4 cups water
1 bay leaf
1 tablespoon beef base

Nolan's Tip: The size of the roast is the most important element in selecting the beef at your grocery store or butcher shop. The goal is to build a relationship with your local butcher. Make him aware of how you like your cuts of beef to be trimmed, the amount of marbling you want in your beef, and how thick you want your beef to ensure consistent cooking every time.

1 Preheat the oven to 300°F.

2 In a small bowl, combine the Dijon mustard, Worcestershire sauce, and chopped garlic.

3 Place the prime rib in a large roasting pan and rub the beef with the mustard sauce. Season the meat with the steak seasoning.

4 Roast the prime rib for 2½ hours. Increase the oven temperature to 400°F and cook until the internal temperature of the beef reaches 115°F (medium-rare) to 120°F (medium), about 30 minutes more.

5 Transfer the beef to a cutting board, upside-down so the juices flow back in, and let it rest for 15 minutes while you make the *jus*.

6 In the same roasting pan, heat the vegetable oil over medium-high heat. Sauté the celery, carrot, and onion until the vegetables are caramelized.

7 Add the water and bring to a boil. Add the bay leaf, reduce the heat, and let simmer for 15 minutes. Stir in the beef base. Strain the *jus* through a fine-mesh sieve into a gravy boat.

8 Flip the prime rib over again and slice it across the grain. Transfer the slices to a platter and drizzle with a little *jus*, passing the remainder separately.

SUNDAY POT ROAST

Texans are particular about the tradition of Sunday family dinner. My family enjoyed this pot roast nearly every Sunday (unless we went with fried chicken). This was the type of dinner I dreamed about while I was playing baseball with my friends in Alvin, Texas. My mom served the pot roast, either after church or on special occasions, with a pan gravy made from the drippings, and all the vegetables were cooked right in the pot. Roasts demand patience and some good cooking technique, as the meat tends to have a milder flavor and is less forgiving of over- or undercooking.

SERVES 8 TO 10
PREP TIME: 20 MINUTES
COOKING TIME: 2 TO 2½ HOURS

4 cups beef broth

4½ cups water

1 tablespoon Worcestershire sauce

2 bay leaves

1 teaspoon kosher salt

1 teaspoon freshly ground black pepper

2 tablespoons vegetable oil

1 (2½- to 3-pound) boneless beef roast (shoulder or round), trimmed on all sides

4 ounces Yukon Gold potatoes

1 pound carrots, peeled and cut into 2-inch pieces

2 medium white onions, cut into wedges

1 celery rib, bias-cut into 1-inch pieces

2 tablespoons unsalted butter, at room temperature

2 tablespoons all-purpose flour

1 Preheat the oven to 300°F.

2 In a medium bowl, combine the beef broth, 1 cup of the water, the Worcestershire sauce, bay leaves, salt, and pepper. Set the sauce aside.

3 Coat the bottom of a heavy roasting pan with the oil, add the meat, and place the pan over medium-high heat to sear the beef. Brown on all sides.

4 Pour the sauce into the pan. Place a sheet of parchment paper over the meat, cover the pan with foil, and roast the meat in the oven for 1 hour.

5 Meanwhile, peel the potatoes and cut into quarters. Rinse the potatoes in cold water for 5 to 10 minutes.

6 After the roast has been cooking for 1 hour, add the potatoes, carrots, onions, and celery to the pan; pour in the remaining 3½ cups water.

7 Cover and cook until the meat is tender, about 1 hour more.

8 Transfer the vegetables to a serving bowl and the meat to a cutting board to rest while you make the gravy.

9 In a deep saucepan set over medium-high heat, stir the butter and flour together to make a roux. Add the liquids from the roasting pan to the saucepan, bring it to a boil, and then reduce the heat and simmer for 10 minutes.

10 Thick-slice the roast and serve with the vegetables and gravy.

SUNDAY BEEF BRAISED IN RED WINE

This is an updated version of my mom's braised beef tips served over white rice, which was a Ryan family staple and a comforting, delicious dish on a cool winter's night. This recipe adds the smoke-rich flavor of pancetta as a big, sharp-breaking curveball against the standard preparation of braised beef. I enjoy both the old and the new ways to cook this family standard.

SERVES 8
PREP TIME: 40 MINUTES
COOKING TIME: 2½ TO 3 HOURS

¼ cup olive oil
1 (6-pound) boneless chuck roast
2 tablespoons kosher salt
1 tablespoon freshly ground black pepper

10 ounces pancetta, chopped
2 large yellow onions, finely chopped
2 large carrots, peeled and finely chopped
4 celery ribs, finely chopped

8 garlic cloves, thinly sliced
8 thyme sprigs
4 rosemary sprigs
¼ cup tomato paste
4 cups dry red wine
4 cups water

1 Preheat the oven to 325°F.

2 Heat the oil in a deep, heavy roasting pan over medium-high heat until it is shimmering but not smoking.

3 Pat the meat dry and season with salt and pepper. Brown the meat in the hot oil on all sides, about 10 minutes. Transfer the meat to a large platter and set aside.

4 Add the pancetta to the oil in the pot and sauté, stirring frequently, until the fat is rendered, about 3 minutes.

5 Add the onions, carrots, and celery and sauté, stirring occasionally, until the vegetables are softened and golden brown, 10 to 12 minutes.

6 Add the garlic, thyme, and rosemary and sauté, stirring vigorously, until the garlic turns golden and soft, about 2 minutes. Stir in the tomato paste and cook for 1 minute.

7 Add the wine to deglaze and boil, stirring occasionally, until the liquid is reduced by half, about 5 minutes. Add the water.

8 Put the meat back in the pan and cover with foil. Transfer to the oven and braise until the meat is tender and the internal temperature reaches 165°F, 2½ to 3 hours.

9 Transfer the meat to a large cutting board. Pour the pan juices into a medium saucepan and boil until reduced by one-third, about 5 minutes.

10 Cut the meat across the grain into ½-inch-thick slices and place in a large serving dish. Pour the sauce over the meat and serve.

Nolan's Serving Tip: Serve with Garlic Mashed Potatoes (page 138) or linguine.

TUSCAN ROAST BEEF

When my mom made roast beef she would place a chuck roast, fat side up, in a shallow roasting pan in the oven, season with salt and pepper, and insert a meat thermometer in the thickest part of the roast. Very straightforward. Chef Cris lends a Tuscan accent to this standard with the addition of extra-virgin olive oil, red wine, and plum tomatoes.

SERVES 8
PREP TIME: 20 MINUTES
COOKING TIME: 3 HOURS

½ cup olive oil

1 (3½-pound) boneless chuck roast, trimmed of fat

1 to 2 teaspoons kosher salt, plus more for the sauce

2 tablespoons freshly ground black pepper, plus more for the sauce

1 pound white mushrooms, quartered

2 carrots, peeled and diced

1 celery rib, diced

1 yellow onion, diced

2 garlic cloves, minced

2 tablespoons chopped fresh curly parsley

1 tablespoon chopped fresh sage

4 cups dry red wine

1 bay leaf

1 (28-ounce) can plum tomatoes, drained, seeds removed

Nolan's Tip: One way to increase the surface area of the meat (for dry rubs and seasoning) is by making ½-inch cuts in a crosshatch pattern.

1 Preheat the oven to 375°F.

2 Heat the oil in a large, heavy roasting pan over medium-high heat until it begins to shimmer—but not to the point where it is smoking.

3 Pat the meat dry with paper towels and season it with salt and pepper. Cook the meat in the hot oil until it is browned on all sides, about 12 minutes. Transfer the meat to a platter.

4 Reduce the heat to medium. Add the mushrooms, carrots, celery, and onion. Cook, stirring occasionally, until all the vegetables turn golden brown and begin to stick to the bottom of the pan, 10 to 12 minutes. Add the garlic, parsley, and sage and stir until the herbs become fragrant and light in color, about 1 minute.

5 Add 1 cup of the wine to deglaze and stir briskly, making sure to lift the caramelized vegetables that are sticking to the pan.

6 When the wine has almost evaporated and thickly coats the vegetables, raise the heat to medium-high and add the remaining 3 cups wine, the bay leaf, and the tomatoes and bring to a boil.

7 Return the roast to the pan and turn to coat it; cover the pot with foil and transfer it to the oven.

8 Cook the meat for 1½ hours. Turn the roast over and ladle some sauce over the top.

9 Cover the pot again and cook until the meat is fork-tender and the internal temperature reaches 165°F, about 1 hour more.

10 Remove the meat from the pot and transfer to a cutting board; tent loosely with foil and let rest while you finish the sauce.

11 Transfer the liquid to a medium saucepan and bring to a boil; reduce until it has a medium-thick consistency. Add salt and pepper to taste.

12 Cut the meat into thick slices (don't be surprised if it falls apart) and place on a warmed serving dish. Cover with sauce and serve.

See photograph on page 88.

SOUTHWEST SUNDAY BREAKFAST WITH BEEF PICADILLO & EGGS

Austin, Texas, is known for its *migas*, a classic Texas brunch item that typically includes eggs, chorizo, onions, fresh chiles, and tortilla chips. This is a new twist on the Austin classic, with Yukon Gold potatoes and ground beef adding just the right counterbalance to the heat from the chorizo. Chef Cris developed this superb brunch dish over the course of his travels through Texas and Mexico.

SERVES 8
PREP TIME: 10 MINUTES
COOKING TIME: 22 TO 25 MINUTES

1½ pounds ground chuck (80-20 meat-to-fat ratio)
8 ounces fresh Mexican chorizo
1 medium yellow onion, diced fine
1 green bell pepper, seeded and diced

1 pound Yukon Gold potatoes, peeled, diced small, and rinsed in cold water
1 tablespoon kosher salt
½ teaspoon ground cumin
¼ teaspoon garlic powder

¼ teaspoon freshly ground black pepper
1½ cups water
1 teaspoon unsalted butter
8 large eggs

---

1 In a large cast-iron skillet, brown the ground chuck and the chorizo over medium heat for 7 to 8 minutes, stirring to break up any lumps. Drain off the fat.

2 Add the onion and pepper and cook until tender, about 3 minutes. Add the potatoes, salt, cumin, garlic powder, pepper, and 1 cup of the water. Stir and cook for 2 minutes.

3 Reduce the heat to low, add the remaining ½ cup water, and cook until the potatoes are tender, 10 to 12 minutes.

4 Meanwhile, heat the butter in a separate skillet and fry the eggs to your liking.

5 Serve the fried eggs on top of the *picadillo*.

5

BEEF
RIBS

BEEF RIBS WITH LAVA MUSTARD BARBECUE SAUCE

Just like a country ham that's dry-cured with salt and sugar and aged to perfection, a good beef rib sauce must balance sweet (in this case brown sugar) with spicy (cayenne and dry mustard). And, as with baby back pork ribs, beef ribs benefit from the added depth and complexity of a rich sauce because they don't have that much flavor to begin with. I promise that your guests will appreciate Chef Cris's Lava Mustard Barbecue Sauce.

SERVES 8
PREP TIME: 5 MINUTES, PLUS 1 DAY TO SEASON THE MEAT
COOKING TIME: 2½ HOURS

---

1 cup brown sugar, packed
2 tablespoons kosher salt
2 tablespoons chili powder
2 teaspoons onion powder

2 teaspoons garlic powder
1 teaspoon freshly ground black pepper
1 teaspoon cayenne pepper

1 teaspoon dry mustard
4 pounds beef ribs
2 cups Lava Mustard Barbecue Sauce (recipe follows)

---

1 Mix all of the seasonings in a small bowl. Rub the mixture over both sides of the beef ribs. Put the ribs in a large roasting pan, cover with foil, and let them sit in the fridge overnight.

2 Preheat the oven to 325°F.

3 Add enough water to the roasting pan to cover the ribs and cover again with foil.

4 Cook the ribs for 1½ hours. Pull the ribs out of the oven and ladle with the juices to keep them moist. Put the ribs back in the oven, cover, and cook for 1 more hour.

5 Preheat the grill to medium and lightly oil the grill grates.

6 Remove the ribs from the oven and baste with some of the barbecue sauce.

7 Finish the ribs on the grill (in batches, if necessary) for 5 minutes on each side—this will ensure that they have a nice crust and smoke-infused flavor. (If you prefer, you can finish them in a 400°F oven.) Serve with the remaining barbecue sauce.

Lava Mustard Barbecue Sauce

Makes about 3 cups
Prep time: 5 minutes

¼ cup unsalted butter
½ yellow onion, finely chopped
¼ cup Kentucky bourbon
1 cup barbecue sauce of your choice
½ cup cider vinegar
½ cup brown sugar, packed
1 tablespoon honey
1 tablespoon dry mustard
1 teaspoon cayenne pepper

1 Melt the butter in a small saucepan over medium heat.

2 Add the onion and sauté for 3 to 4 minutes, but don't allow the onion to turn brown. Add the bourbon and cook off the alcohol, 1 to 2 minutes.

3 Add the barbecue sauce, vinegar, brown sugar, honey, mustard, and cayenne. Simmer for 30 minutes, stirring at regular intervals.

BEEF SHORT RIBS WITH MOLE SAUCE

In this recipe, Chef Cris takes a classic *mole* (Mexican chocolate) sauce and turns mundane beef ribs into a gourmet Mexican BBQ dish. My son Reese has seen Cris work miracles using simple and fresh ingredients to cater business lunches for the R Bank (owned by the Ryan family) or the Round Rock Express (the AAA minor-league affiliate of the Rangers owned by Ryan-Saunders Baseball).

SERVES 8
PREP TIME: 5 MINUTES
COOKING TIME: 1 HOUR 45 MINUTES

8 racks beef short ribs
1 large yellow onion, diced
2 tablespoons Worcestershire sauce

2 tablespoons kosher salt
2 tablespoons freshly ground black pepper

4 bay leaves
8 cups (2 quarts) water
1 (16-ounce) jar *mole* sauce

1 Fill a large stockpot with water and bring to a boil over high heat. Reduce the heat to medium and add the ribs, onion, Worcestershire, salt, pepper, and bay leaves. Cook until the ribs are fall-off-the-bone tender, about 90 minutes.

2 Preheat the oven to 350°F.

3 Transfer the ribs to a large roasting pan and cover with foil to keep warm.

4 Empty out the stockpot and add the water and *mole* sauce. Cook over high heat until blended to a smooth consistency. Remove from the heat and set aside.

5 Cover the ribs with the *mole* sauce, cover with foil, and bake for 15 minutes.

Nolan's Serving Tip: Serve the ribs with Garlic Mashed Potatoes (page 138) for a nice balance of flavor and texture.

REESE: "Cris is such a talented chef—I can ask him to cater a lunch or dinner for a large group of bankers or baseball execs, and he will produce a world-class menu of dishes that reflect the unique approach to Tex-Mex cuisine on display in this cookbook."

BEER-BRAISED COUNTRY RIBS

There's always a debate going on about which is better: beef ribs or pork ribs. There's no easy way to pick a favorite, other than to say that they are both delicious if you cook them properly based on their unique qualities. I will seek out a restaurant that has a reputation for making St. Louis–style pork ribs that have a sweet, spicy sauce and are fall-off-the-bone tender. I also love to grill beef ribs when I'm at home with the family and I can try one of Chef Cris's new sauce recipes. Beef ribs really let you taste the smoke on the meat.

I am not likely to order ribs off the menu at a restaurant, though, as they are too much of a challenge to eat. I don't enjoy fighting with my food at a restaurant. For the same reason, I don't see beef ribs as good ballpark food.

In this recipe, we use beer, Worcestershire sauce, barbecue sauce, and steak sauce to marinate the ribs before putting them through the braising process. Braising, used most often for less tender cuts such as brisket and pot roast, relies on a small amount of liquid (in this case beer) to create fork-tender beef ribs.

SERVES 8
PREP TIME: 5 MINUTES
COOKING TIME: 2½ TO 3 HOURS

---

2 (12-ounce) bottles dark beer
2½ cups barbecue sauce of your choice

½ cup Worcestershire sauce
½ cup steak sauce of your choice
4 pounds beef ribs, racks cut in half

2 yellow onions, sliced
2 cups water

---

1 Preheat the oven to 350°F.

2 In a large roasting pan, combine 1 bottle of beer, 1¼ cups of the barbecue sauce, the Worcestershire sauce, and the steak sauce.

3 Place the ribs in the pan and turn them to cover with the marinade. Let them sit at room temperature for 15 minutes.

4 Coat a heavy cast-iron skillet with a light coat of nonstick olive oil spray. Sear the ribs over high heat until light brown, about 3 minutes per side.

5 Return the ribs to the roasting pan with the marinade, scatter the onions around the ribs, and pour in the water and remaining bottle of beer.

6 Place a sheet of parchment paper over the ribs and cover the pan with foil.

7 Bake until the ribs are tender, 1½ to 2 hours.

8 Uncover the pan and ladle the pan juices over the ribs. Slather the ribs with the remaining 1¼ cups barbecue sauce and bake, uncovered, until the rib meat is brown and the sauce is nice and thick, about 1 more hour.

Nolan's Serving Tip: These beef ribs go great with my Loaded Yukon Gold Smashed Potatoes (page 137).

GRILLED ASIAN BEEF RIBS

My goal with ribs is to cook them until they are tender, use a sauce that's moist and flavorful, and make sure that the result keeps the guests coming back asking me to throw more racks on the charcoal. This recipe leans on Asian ingredients (soy sauce, mirin, rice vinegar, and sesame oil) and blends savory (garlic and soy sauce) with sweet (brown sugar and sweet chili sauce) to strike the perfect balance of flavors with fall-off-the-bone texture.

Rusty Staub, one of the best pinch hitters in baseball history, was a successful chef and restaurateur who had a famous recipe for Louisiana ribs that put his restaurant on the culinary map back in the 1970s and '80s. The secret was the moistness of the ribs and the smoke and sweetness of the sauce. In this recipe, Chef Cris gives you the same type of eating experience that people enjoyed at Rusty's restaurant in New York City.

SERVES 8
PREP TIME: 5 MINUTES, PLUS 1 DAY TO MARINATE THE MEAT
COOKING TIME: 20 TO 22 MINUTES

1 cup soy sauce
½ cup mirin (Japanese rice wine)
½ cup dark brown sugar, packed

¼ cup unseasoned rice vinegar
¼ cup toasted sesame oil
¼ cup minced garlic

2 large scallions, chopped
8 racks beef ribs
½ cup sweet chili sauce (we use Mae Ploy brand)

1 In a medium bowl, whisk together the soy sauce, mirin, brown sugar, rice vinegar, sesame oil, garlic, and scallions. Pour the sauce into a large roasting pan, add the ribs, and cover with foil or plastic wrap. Marinate overnight in the fridge.

2 Preheat the grill to medium and lightly oil the grill grates.

3 Drain the ribs and discard the marinade. Grill the ribs until browned and cooked to medium-rare, 10 to 12 minutes per side.

4 Serve the ribs with the sweet chili sauce on the side.

6

BRISKET, FLANK STEAK

& FLAT IRON STEAK

BARBACOA BRISKET

I did not have brisket growing up—my mom never prepared it. Brisket was introduced to the consumer market primarily as a way for the meatpacking houses to be able to utilize all parts of the animal. It comes down to adding value. Same thing with flank steak: I can remember when flank steak started showing up in markets in the 1970s and '80s and the only people in Texas who bought it were Mexican chefs who knew how to take this lesser cut and make it flavorful with an array of spices and marinades. The cultural and culinary traditions of Mexicans living in South Texas crossed over into the mainstream in the 1980s and '90s with the growing popularity of fajitas, carne asada tacos, stews, and casseroles.

SERVES 6 TO 8
PREP TIME: 5 MINUTES
COOKING TIME: 4½ HOURS

---

1 (9- to 11-pound) whole brisket
1 recipe Guajillo Pepper Paste
   (recipe follows)

¼ cup vegetable oil
1 large onion
2 garlic cloves, peeled

3 bay leaves
1 tablespoon apple cider vinegar
1 teaspoon kosher salt

---

1 Preheat the oven to 350°F.

2 Rub the brisket all over with the guajillo pepper paste.

3 In a large roasting pan, heat the oil over high heat and sear the brisket for about 5 minutes per side.

4 Cover the roasting pan with foil and cook in the oven for 3 hours and 15 minutes.

5 Transfer the brisket to a stockpot and add enough water to cover the brisket. Add the onion, garlic, bay leaves, vinegar, and salt.

6 Bring to a boil over high heat and boil for 5 minutes. Reduce the heat and simmer for 1 hour.

7 Use two forks to pull the brisket apart and serve.

Guajillo Pepper Paste

Makes about 2 cups
Prep time: 30 minutes

9 dried ancho chiles, stemmed and seeded
5 dried guajillo chiles, stemmed and seeded
2½ cups water
4 garlic cloves, peeled
½ large onion, cut into chunks
½ teaspoon dried Mexican oregano
1½ teaspoons kosher salt

1 Heat a large skillet over medium-high heat for 2 minutes.

2 Add the ancho and guajillo chiles and cook, pressing with a metal spatula and turning occasionally, until they blister, about 30 seconds.

3 Transfer the peppers to a medium saucepan and add the water, garlic, onion, oregano, and salt.

4 Bring to a boil over high heat and boil for 5 minutes. Reduce the heat and simmer until the peppers become tender, about 20 minutes.

5 Transfer the mixture to a blender and puree until smooth.

6 Store the paste in a covered container in the refrigerator until you are ready to use it.

BIG TEX BRISKET PATTY MELT

My take on the classic patty melt—a burger with cheese on toasted bread rather than a hamburger bun—packs in the flavor with shredded smoked brisket, smoked bacon, ground beef, Kentucky bourbon, pepper jack cheese, and Texas toast.

This dish brings me back to my trips to Kansas City while pitching for the California Angels and Texas Rangers. We used to visit Gates Bar-B-Q, where they would cook brisket low and slow to perfection. Kansas City was always one of my favorite restaurant towns while I was pitching in the American League, and I still enjoy my visits to KC to explore new places for steak or brisket.

Here in Texas, one of the best places to enjoy brisket is Rudy's Bar-B-Q, where you can order the meat lean or regular. If you get the lean brisket the sauce is probably essential, because the meat does not have much flavor on its own; with the regular brisket, though, you can skip the sauce because the meat has big flavor thanks to the fat content. This patty melt is a unique and intriguing blend of brisket and ground chuck, the ultimate dish to impress your friends and family.

SERVES 8
PREP TIME: 30 MINUTES
COOKING TIME: 10 MINUTES

---

1 pound smoked brisket, chopped
2 tablespoons unsalted butter
2 tablespoons vegetable oil
3 yellow onions, sliced thin
16 slices smoked bacon

4 pounds ground chuck (80-20 meat-to-fat ratio)
3 tablespoons Nolan Ryan Steak Seasoning (page 25)
16 slices Texas Toast (page 37)

8 slices white cheddar cheese
8 slices pepper jack cheese
1 recipe Kentucky Bourbon BBQ Sauce (recipe follows)

---

1 Preheat the grill to high and the oven to its lowest setting. Lightly oil the grill grates.

2 Warm the brisket in a small roasting pan in the oven.

3 Melt the butter and oil in a large cast-iron skillet over medium-high heat. Cook the onions until golden brown. Transfer the onions to a plate and tent with foil to keep warm.

4 Cook the bacon in the same skillet until crisp. Transfer the bacon to a plate lined with paper towels and tent with foil to keep warm.

5 Form the ground chuck into 16 patties. Season the patties with the steak seasoning and pepper.

6 Grill the patties (in batches, if necessary) for 5 minutes per side and transfer to a platter.

7 Place the Texas toast on the grill. Cover each with a slice of cheese and allow it to melt evenly.

8 To form each patty melt, place 1 beef patty, 2 slices bacon, some brisket, and some onions on a slice of cheddar cheese–covered toast. Spoon on some BBQ sauce and cover the patty with a slice of pepper jack–covered toast.

Kentucky Bourbon BBQ Sauce

Makes 2 cups
Prep time: 10 minutes

½ cup Kentucky bourbon
1 teaspoon Dijon mustard
1 teaspoon freshly ground black pepper
1 teaspoon adobo sauce (from a can of chipotle peppers
in adobo sauce)
1 teaspoon honey
1¾ cups barbecue sauce of your choice

1 Pour the bourbon into a deep saucepan and flame it to burn off the alcohol—take care not to get too close to the pan!

2 Let the bourbon simmer over high heat until half of the liquid has evaporated.

3 Stir in the Dijon mustard, pepper, adobo, and honey. Add the barbecue sauce and stir with a whisk.

4 Cook on low heat for 2 to 3 minutes.

ADOBO & BEER–BRAISED BRISKET

The nutty, toasty, and rich flavors of beer and adobo (the liquid from canned chipotle peppers) are key elements in many Mexican dishes, and in this brisket recipe they combine perfectly with the guajillo peppers, onions, beef broth, and cider vinegar.

Brisket has gotten really popular as a BBQ item here in Texas. When I go to Cooper's Old Time Pit Bar-B-Que in Llano, they have a pit with lots of great choices: beef ribs, brisket, chopped beef, rib-eye, prime rib, sirloin, and T-bone, as well as *cabrito* (goat kid) and chicken. I usually get five slices of brisket and two other meats.

SERVES 8 TO 10
PREP TIME: 20 MINUTES, PLUS 1 DAY TO MARINATE THE MEAT
COOKING TIME: 4 HOURS

---

1 whole brisket, trimmed of excess fat
1 recipe Guajillo Pepper Paste (page 110)
1 cup olive oil

6 large yellow onions, cut into thick rings
1 bay leaf
2 cups beef broth

1 (12-ounce) bottle dark beer
¼ cup cider vinegar
Kosher salt and freshly ground black pepper to taste

---

1 Place the brisket in a large roasting pan and rub it on all sides with the guajillo pepper paste. Cover the pan with foil and let it sit in the refrigerator overnight to infuse the flavor into the meat.

2 Preheat the oven to 375°F.

3 Transfer the brisket to a platter momentarily. Heat ½ cup of the olive oil in the roasting pan over medium heat until the first wisp of smoke rises.

4 Return the brisket to the roasting pan and sear it on all sides until it turns a nice golden brown, 10 to 12 minutes per side.

5 Transfer the brisket to the platter again.

6 Heat the remaining ½ cup olive oil over medium heat. Add the onions and bay leaf and cook for 10 minutes, stirring occasionally.

7 Transfer half of the sautéed onions to a bowl and reserve.

8 Place the brisket on the onions remaining in the pan, and then top with the reserved onions. Pour in the beef broth, beer, and vinegar; the liquid should come about halfway up the sides of the meat.

9 Cover the pan with foil and place it in the oven. Cook, basting every 30 minutes with the beer broth, until the brisket is tender and the internal temperature reaches 155°F, about 3½ hours.

10 Remove the pan from the oven. Turn the brisket upside-down so the juices flow back in, and let it rest in the pan for 15 minutes.

11 Transfer the brisket to a cutting board, right side up.

12 Skim off any fat from the sauce and season with salt and pepper. Pour or ladle the sauce into a bowl.

13 Slice the meat across the grain and serve with the sauce.

BEEF SATAY WITH PINEAPPLE MARINADE

At the end of a long day at work at the ranch, this charred steak cooked with skewers on the grill is the perfect way to finish on a high note. The wonderfully pungent flavors of sherry, hoisin sauce, soy sauce, ginger, and pineapple juice combine perfectly with the smokiness of the grilled flank steak. Think of this beef satay as an appetizer course before my Summer Grilled Tenderloin of Beef with Spicy Crab and Avocado Salad (page 125) or Cobb Salad with Sirloin (page 130).

MAKES 16 TO 20 SKEWERS
PREP TIME: 10 MINUTES, PLUS 2 HOURS TO MARINATE THE MEAT
COOKING TIME: 6 MINUTES

½ cup pineapple juice
⅓ cup soy sauce
¼ cup dry sherry

1½ tablespoons hoisin sauce
¼ cup chopped scallions
1 teaspoon grated ginger

2 pounds flank steak, trimmed of all fat

1 In a large glass baking dish, combine the pineapple juice, soy sauce, sherry, hoisin sauce, scallions, and ginger. Set aside ¼ cup of the marinade in a small bowl, cover, and refrigerate to use later for basting.

2 Cut the flank steaks across the grain on a diagonal into ¼-inch-thick slices. Place the steak slices in the marinade and turn to coat well. Cover and marinate in the fridge for 2 hours.

3 Preheat the grill to high and lightly oil the grill grates. Soak 16 to 20 wooden skewers in water for at least 10 minutes.

4 Drain the steak and discard the marinade. Thread the steak slices onto the skewers.

5 Grill the skewers (in batches, if necessary) for 3 minutes per side, brushing periodically with the reserved marinade.

EASY FLANK STEAK SANDWICH ON SOURDOUGH TOAST

I discovered sourdough on my baseball road trips to the Bay Area, while pitching for the Astros against the San Francisco Giants. San Francisco is probably the best restaurant city in the United States, and I really enjoy the Dungeness crab and sourdough bread. I probably consume more than I should, but it is one of the true pleasures of dining out in San Francisco.

For me, sourdough toast is the perfect sandwich bread—just the right texture and flavor to complement the flank steak, sliced avocado, lettuce, and tomato.

MAKES 8 SANDWICHES
PREP TIME: 5 MINUTES
COOKING TIME: 10 TO 14 MINUTES

2 pounds flank steak, trimmed of all fat
4 teaspoons vegetable oil
4 teaspoons Nolan Ryan Steak Seasoning (page 25)

16 slices fresh sourdough bread
4 avocados, peeled, pitted, and sliced thin
1 head iceberg lettuce, shredded

2 large tomatoes, sliced thin
2 large red onions, sliced thin
1 recipe Sriracha Aioli (recipe follows)

1 Preheat the grill to medium-high and lightly oil the grill grates.

2 Rub the steaks all over with the oil and steak seasoning.

3 Cook the steaks (in batches, if necessary) for 5 to 7 minutes per side for medium-rare. Transfer the steaks to a cutting board to rest for 10 minutes.

4 Place the sourdough slices on the grill and toast until light brown on both sides.

5 Cut the steaks diagonally across the grain into thin strips.

6 Make the steak sandwiches with avocado, lettuce, tomato, and onion, and top with sriracha aioli.

See photograph on page 108.

Sriracha Aioli

Makes about ½ cup
Prep time: 5 minutes

6 tablespoons mayonnaise
2 tablespoons sriracha hot sauce
2 teaspoons freshly ground black pepper

Mix all of the ingredients in a small bowl, cover, and chill in the fridge until ready to use.

GRILLED BALSAMIC FLANK STEAK

This is strictly an outdoor dinner-party type of dish—something to put on the grill when the weather is nice and the beer is cold. Keep it simple! The balsamic vinegar, olive oil, and beef broth add acidity and depth to the marinated flank steak.

SERVES 8 TO 10
PREP TIME: 20 MINUTES, PLUS 4 HOURS TO MARINATE THE MEAT
COOKING TIME: 12 TO 16 MINUTES

1⅔ cups olive oil
⅓ cup balsamic vinegar
2 yellow onions, sliced thin
2 garlic cloves, minced
1 tablespoon chopped fresh parsley

1 tablespoon chopped fresh cilantro
1 tablespoon kosher salt
1 tablespoon freshly ground black pepper
1½ teaspoons smoked paprika
3½ pounds flank steak, trimmed of all fat

2 cups beef broth
½ cup dry red wine
1 teaspoon sugar
2 teaspoons unsalted butter

1 Combine ⅔ cup of the olive oil with the balsamic vinegar and mix well. Transfer half of this vinaigrette to a small bowl and set aside.

2 Pour the remaining vinaigrette and the remaining 1 cup olive oil into a large glass baking dish. Add the onions, garlic, parsley, cilantro, salt, and pepper, and paprika and stir well to combine.

3 Lay the steak in the pan and flip it a few times to ensure that it is covered with the marinade. Cover and place in the fridge for 4 hours—turn the steak once per hour to make sure both sides are coated.

4 In a saucepan, bring the beef broth, wine, sugar, and reserved vinaigrette to a boil over medium-high heat. Reduce the heat to a simmer for 10 minutes and add the butter. Stir to combine and remove from the heat; cover to keep warm.

5 Preheat the grill to high and lightly oil the grill grates.

6 Remove the steak from the marinade and cook for 6 to 8 minutes per side for medium-rare. Transfer the steak to a cutting board to rest for 10 minutes.

7 Slice the flank steak across the grain and serve with the sauce on the side.

Nolan's Serving Tip: Spinach Casserole (page 142) is the ideal vegetable side dish to complement the sweet and tart flavors of the sauce.

COWBOY STEAK WITH POBLANO PEPPER SAUCE

Poblano peppers are a natural pairing with flat iron steak—the cut that I like to use for cowboy steaks cooked in a cast-iron skillet over an open fire. My view on peppers is that they add highlights of flavor, but they should never overpower the pure taste of the cut of beef. The flat iron steak is from two layers of the top blade, off the shoulder of the animal, and has had all the connective tissue removed. When sliced thin, you see significant marbling. This is one of the most versatile cuts of beef—you can cook it in a variety of ways, it is really tender, and it is also inexpensive.

SERVES 4
PREP TIME: 25 MINUTES
COOKING TIME: 16 MINUTES

---

2 tablespoons olive oil

3 poblano peppers, seeded and minced

1½ medium yellow onions, sliced

3 garlic cloves, chopped

2 tablespoons chili powder

1 tablespoon kosher salt, plus more for seasoning the meat

1 teaspoon crushed red pepper

2 plum tomatoes, chopped

½ cup water

½ bunch fresh cilantro, chopped (leaves only)

Freshly ground black pepper

4 (6- to 8-ounce) flat iron steaks

---

1 Heat the oil in a large cast-iron skillet over medium-high heat. At the point where a drop of water will sizzle in the oil, add the poblano peppers and onions and sauté for 3 minutes.

2 Add the garlic, 1 tablespoon of the chili powder, and the salt and crushed red pepper. Cook until the onions are tender, about 4 minutes, and then stir in the tomatoes.

3 Add the water and half of the cilantro and stir; reduce the sauce for 10 minutes, adding black pepper to taste.

4 Keep the sauce on low heat on the stovetop while you cook the steaks.

5 Preheat the grill or a cast-iron skillet to high. If using a grill, lightly oil the grill grates.

6 Rub the steak with the remaining 1 tablespoon chili powder and additional salt and pepper to taste.

7 Grill or pan-sear the steaks (in batches, if necessary) for approximately 8 minutes per side for medium-rare. Transfer the steaks to a cutting board to rest for 5 to 7 minutes.

8 Serve with the poblano pepper sauce and garnish with the remaining cilantro.

COFFEE COWBOY STEAK

The key to this recipe is the coffee, which adds an interesting flavor to the meat. Much like red-eye gravy on ham, though, the coffee always stays in the background to allow the perfectly cooked flat iron to steal the show.

A lot of people ask me about the history of flat iron steaks, and the truth is that they were invented by the National Cattlemen's Beef Association. In 2002, the NCBA commissioned a muscle profiling study in an effort to find better, more efficient cuts from the chuck and round for retail and food-service use. In this study (a joint venture between the NCBA's Center for Research and Technical Services, the University of Florida, and the University of Nebraska), every major muscle of the steer was analyzed separately for flavor and tenderness. The study found that the flat iron is second only to the tenderloin in terms of tenderness. This revelation pushed the flat iron steak into the starring role in the NCBA's "Value Cuts" promotional campaign.

SERVES 4
PREP TIME: 5 MINUTES, PLUS 20 MINUTES TO SEASON THE MEAT
COOKING TIME: 16 TO 18 MINUTES

---

1 tablespoon coffee beans
1 tablespoon whole white peppercorns
1 tablespoon Old Bay seasoning

1½ teaspoons garlic powder
1½ teaspoons kosher salt
1 teaspoon paprika

4 (6- to 8-ounce) flat iron steaks
1½ tablespoons olive oil
1 tablespoon Worcestershire sauce

---

1 Place the coffee beans, peppercorns, Old Bay, garlic powder, salt, and paprika in a coffee grinder. Grind until the ingredients form a fine powder. Rub the spice mix on both sides of the flat iron steaks. Set aside at room temperature for 20 minutes.

2 Preheat the grill or a cast-iron skillet to high. If using a grill, lightly oil the grill grates.

3 In a small bowl, combine the olive oil and Worcestershire sauce and brush the steaks with the mixture.

4 Grill or pan-sear the steaks (in batches, if necessary) for 8 to 9 minutes per side, brushing the steaks with the oil and Worcestershire when turning.

Nolan's Serving Tip: Serve the Coffee Cowboy Steak with my Traditional Green Bean Casserole (page 141) for the ideal pairing.

7

SALADS &
SIDES

LONE STAR PECAN APPLE SALAD

This summer/autumn salad is composed only of green apples, celery, and pecans, tossed in a dressing made from lemon juice, honey, mayonnaise, and sour cream. Pecans are one of my favorite nuts—they have much more flavor than walnuts and the texture is perfect on its own, without being candied or spiced. I enjoy the tartness of the green apple, which adds a nice contrast to the dish. And the dressing gives this salad a light, velvety texture.

SERVES 8 TO 10
PREP TIME: 10 MINUTES

1½ pounds tart green apples, diced
2 teaspoons fresh lemon juice
2 medium celery ribs, finely chopped

½ cup pecans
4 to 6 tablespoons mayonnaise
2 tablespoons sour cream

2 tablespoons honey
1 teaspoon kosher salt

1 Place the apples in a large bowl with the lemon juice and just enough water to cover the apples. Drain the apples and return them to the bowl. Add the chopped celery and pecans.

2 Combine the mayonnaise, sour cream, honey, and salt in a small bowl. Add the mixture to the apples, celery, and pecans, folding them into the dressing.

3 Cover and chill in the refrigerator until ready to serve.

SUMMER GRILLED TENDERLOIN OF BEEF WITH SPICY CRAB & AVOCADO SALAD

Tenderloin, crab, and avocado make a great combination. This surf-and-turf salad doubles as a hearty appetizer or an elegant lunch dish. The briny sweetness of the crab goes perfectly with the grilled tenderloin.

SERVES 4
PREP TIME: 15 MINUTES, PLUS 15 MINUTES TO MARINATE THE MEAT
COOKING TIME: 14 MINUTES

For the salad:
4 vine-ripened tomatoes, diced
½ red onion, finely chopped
¼ bunch cilantro, chopped (leaves only)
Juice of 1 lemon
Juice of 1 lime
1 tablespoon jalapeño juice (from jarred pickled jalapeños)

1 tablespoon hot sauce
1 tablespoon kosher salt
1 tablespoon freshly ground black pepper
1 pound lump crabmeat (remove all bones and shells—or ask your fishmonger to perform this task)
3 large avocados, peeled, pitted, and sliced thin

For the steak:
¼ cup olive oil
¼ cup balsamic vinegar
2 shallots, chopped
2 tablespoons Nolan Ryan Steak Seasoning (page 25)
4 (7-ounce) tenderloin steaks, 1 inch thick

Nolan's Tip: The USDA identifies four grades of crabmeat: jumbo lump, backfin lump, flake white, and claw. Buy the best crabmeat available—jumbo or backfin lump—for this recipe. Look for fresh crabmeat at a fish market or at the fish counter of your local grocery store.

1 First, make the salad. In a large bowl, combine the tomatoes, red onion, cilantro, lemon juice, lime juice, jalapeño juice, hot sauce, salt, and pepper.

2 Add the crabmeat and avocado and toss gently, trying not to break up the crab and avocado. Cover and chill in the fridge while you cook the steaks.

3 Preheat the grill to high and lightly oil the grill grates.

4 In a large glass baking dish, combine the olive oil, balsamic vinegar, shallots, and steak seasoning. Add the steaks, turning to coat, and set aside to marinate for 15 minutes.

5 Remove the steaks from the marinade and grill (in batches, if necessary) for 7 minutes per side for medium-rare.

6 To serve, place a grilled tenderloin at the center of each plate and arrange the crab-avocado salad on top of and around the steak.

CITRUS-INFUSED AVOCADO SALAD WITH TORTILLA CHIPS

In this salad—one of my favorites—Chef Cris pairs citrus flavors (orange and lime juice) with the sweetness of honey and the bite of fresh cilantro. Roma tomatoes are always available at the grocery store, so you can enjoy this summer-style salad year-round. Chef Cris often bakes his own tortilla chips, but you can use store-bought chips and you'll still really enjoy all of these fresh flavors.

SERVES 10
PREP TIME: 10 MINUTES, PLUS 1 HOUR TO CHILL

⅔ cup olive oil
½ cup fresh orange juice
⅓ cup red wine vinegar
Juice of 2 limes
1 tablespoon honey

2 bunches cilantro, chopped (leaves only)
10 large avocados, peeled, pitted, and diced
8 large Roma tomatoes, cut into ¾-inch dice

1 teaspoon kosher salt
1 teaspoon freshly ground black pepper
1 (1-pound) bag tortilla chips

1 Mix the olive oil, orange juice, vinegar, lime juice, honey, and cilantro in a large bowl. Add the avocado, tomatoes, salt, and pepper. Mix gently. Cover and chill in the refrigerator for 1 hour.

2 Serve with the tortilla chips.

FETA & TOMATO SALAD WITH GREEK VINAIGRETTE

This take on a classic Greek salad is one of Ruth's favorite summer salads.

SERVES 6
PREP TIME: 10 MINUTES

1 heart of romaine lettuce, cut into 1-inch chunks

1 recipe Greek Vinaigrette (recipe follows)

8 Roma tomatoes, diced

2 to 3 cucumbers, peeled and diced

2 to 3 red bell peppers, seeded and diced

½ cup capers

½ cup minced scallions

1 red onion, finely diced

1 cup crumbled feta cheese

1 Toss the salad greens in a large bowl with half of the vinaigrette until the leaves are coated. Divide the dressed leaves among six serving plates.

2 In a medium bowl, toss the tomatoes, cucumbers, peppers, capers, and scallions with the remaining half of the vinaigrette. Place the tomato-cucumber mixture on top of the greens.

3 Garnish with the red onion and feta cheese just before serving.

Greek Vinaigrette

Makes 2 cups
Prep time: 5 minutes

1½ cups extra-virgin olive oil

1 cup fresh lemon juice

2 tablespoons chopped fresh oregano

1 tablespoon kosher salt

1 tablespoon freshly ground black pepper

Mix all of the ingredients in a blender until smooth. Keep the dressing at room temperature until ready to serve.

COBB SALAD WITH SIRLOIN

Sirloin and flat iron steaks are ideal for Cobb salads—they have a bold flavor and are easy to thin-slice for the perfect texture alongside the tomatoes, lettuce, bacon, avocados, and hard-boiled eggs. I use a creamy vinaigrette or a traditional ranch dressing to go with my Cobb salad with sirloin. This makes a satisfying lunch when I'm not in the mood for a heavier meal during a busy workday.

SERVES 4
PREP TIME: 20 MINUTES
COOKING TIME: 8 MINUTES

---

12 slices bacon
2 pounds sirloin steaks, 1 inch thick
1 teaspoon kosher salt
1 teaspoon freshly ground black pepper

2 heads Romaine lettuce, cut into 1-inch chunks
6 plum tomatoes, sliced
3 avocados, peeled, pitted, and sliced thin

8 ounces sharp cheddar cheese, shredded
6 hard-boiled eggs, chopped
1 cup chopped scallions
Creamy dressing of your choice

Nolan's Tip: Don't slice the avocados until you are ready to serve the salad. This way, the avocados won't turn brown by the time the plates arrive at the table.

1 Cook the bacon in a frying pan over high heat until crisp. Pat the bacon dry with paper towels. Dice the bacon and set aside.

2 Preheat the grill to high and lightly oil the grill grates.

3 Season the steaks with salt and pepper. Grill the steaks (in batches, if necessary) for 4 minutes per side for medium-rare. Transfer the steaks to a cutting board to rest for 10 minutes, then slice into thin strips.

4 Place the salad ingredients in a large bowl in the following order: lettuce, tomato, steak, avocado, bacon, shredded cheese, chopped egg, scallions. Serve with your favorite salad dressing.

RUTH RYAN'S CHILLED ASPARAGUS & MOZZARELLA PLATTER

This recipe includes toasted pecans for crunch, lemon juice for a hint of acid, brown sugar for sweetness, and cider vinegar for that "wow" factor that ties it all together.

SERVES 8
PREP TIME: 10 MINUTES, PLUS 2½ HOURS TO CHILL

⅔ cup light brown sugar, packed
⅔ cup cider vinegar
⅔ cup soy sauce

4 teaspoons fresh lemon juice
1 teaspoon garlic powder
2 pounds fresh asparagus, trimmed

1½ pounds fresh mozzarella, sliced
⅔ cup olive oil
1 cup toasted pecans

1 In a saucepan, combine the brown sugar, vinegar, soy sauce, lemon juice, and garlic powder. Bring to a boil over medium-high heat. Reduce the heat and simmer for 5 minutes. Remove from the heat and set aside for a few minutes; then, place in the fridge until cool, about 30 minutes.

2 Bring a large saucepan of water to a boil over high heat. Add the asparagus, reduce the heat, and simmer until tender, 3 to 5 minutes, depending on the thickness of the asparagus. Drain and rinse the asparagus in ice-cold water to slow the cooking and bring out their beautiful color.

3 Place the asparagus in a large zip-top bag, cover with the chilled marinade, and seal the bag. Refrigerate for 2 hours.

4 Drain the asparagus from the marinade and place the asparagus in the center of a large serving dish. Arrange the fresh mozzarella around the edges of the plate and drizzle with the olive oil.

5 Garnish with the toasted pecans and serve.

POTATOES AU GRATIN

I love crispy potatoes, and this side dish covers all the comfort-food bases: cheesy, salty, and pepper-packed. Serve with the Rib-Eye with Sriracha-Soy Marinade (page 52) or the Grilled BBQ T-bone with Kentucky Bourbon (page 56) and you will hit a home run every time.

SERVES 8 TO 10
PREP TIME: 15 MINUTES
COOKING TIME: 1 HOUR

2¼ pounds Idaho potatoes, peeled and sliced ⅛-inch thick
½ cup (¼ pound) unsalted butter
2 cups whole milk

2 cups heavy cream
1 tablespoon kosher salt
1 tablespoon freshly ground black pepper

1 pinch ground nutmeg
6 ounces Swiss cheese, grated
4 ounces Parmesan cheese, grated
½ cup fine bread crumbs

---

1 Preheat the oven to 350°F. Lightly grease a 9- by 13-inch baking dish.

2 Bring a large pot of water to a boil over high heat and cook the potatoes for about 15 minutes—you want them cooked just halfway through. Drain the potatoes, place them in a large bowl, and let cool in the fridge.

3 In a medium saucepan, melt the butter over medium heat. Add the milk, heavy cream, salt, pepper, and nutmeg and let simmer for 5 minutes, and then remove from the heat.

4 Layer the potatoes in the baking dish, alternating them with the grated cheese. Top with the cream and milk mixture, then top with more cheese. Place a sheet of parchment paper over the potatoes and cover the dish with foil.

5 Bake until the potatoes are fully cooked, 30 to 45 minutes. If you insert a paring knife in the middle, it should come out almost clean.

6 Increase the oven temperature to 400°F. Remove the parchment and foil and sprinkle the bread crumbs over the top. Bake, uncovered, until the cheese is golden brown and a crust has formed, about 5 minutes.

LOADED YUKON GOLD SMASHED POTATOES

This recipe improves upon the usual loaded baked potato (typically smothered with bacon, cheese, and sour cream) by adding French-fried onions and scallions as a flavor-packed double-play combination. Joe's Bar-B-Q in Alvin, Texas, loads up its baked potatoes with smoked brisket—one of my all-time favorite lunches!

This dish goes great with my Beer-Braised Country Ribs (page 104) and the Wild Mushroom and Cranberry–Stuffed Tenderloin (page 68).

SERVES 8
PREP TIME: 15 MINUTES
COOKING TIME: 30 MINUTES

10 slices bacon
12 small Yukon Gold potatoes
2 tablespoons olive oil
1 teaspoon kosher salt

1 teaspoon freshly ground black pepper
1½ cups store-bought French-fried onions

8 ounces cheddar cheese, shredded
¾ cup sour cream
1 to 2 teaspoons minced scallions

1 Preheat the oven to 425°F.

2 Cook the bacon in a frying pan over high heat until crisp. Pat the bacon dry with paper towels. Crumble the bacon and set aside.

3 Bring a large pot of water to a boil over high heat. Add the potatoes and cook until three-quarters done, about 15 minutes. Drain and set aside to cool.

4 Brush the potatoes with the oil and season with salt and pepper. Place them in a baking dish and bake until fully cooked, about 15 minutes.

5 Smash the potatoes with a potato masher or a large meat fork. Top with the crumbled bacon, fried onions, and cheese. Bake until the cheese melts, about 5 minutes.

6 Add dollops of sour cream on top, garnish with scallions, and serve.

GARLIC MASHED POTATOES

This is one of those standards that never goes out of style. The cracked black pepper adds balance to all the cream and butter, and there's just enough salt to offset the tang of the roasted garlic. Why not enjoy these with the Big Tex Rib-Eye with Adobo Butter (page 44) or the Beef Short Ribs with *Mole* Sauce (page 103)?

SERVES 6
PREP TIME: 20 MINUTES
COOKING TIME: 10 MINUTES

1½ pounds Yukon Gold potatoes, peeled and sliced into ¼-inch rounds

1 garlic clove, smashed
½ cup heavy cream
6 tablespoons unsalted butter, melted

2 tablespoons kosher salt
2 tablespoons cracked black pepper

---

1 Preheat the oven to 350°F.

2 Bring a medium saucepan of salted water to a rolling boil over high heat. Add the potatoes and cook until fork-tender, 8 to 10 minutes. Drain the potatoes and set them aside.

3 Meanwhile, place the garlic in a small baking dish and roast for 10 minutes.

4 In a small saucepan, bring the cream to a boil over medium heat, but do not let it curdle. Remove the pan from the heat as soon as it comes to a boil.

5 Using a potato masher or a large meat fork, mash the potatoes; whip in the melted butter, cream, roasted garlic, salt, and pepper. Keep mashing until the potatoes are smooth and fluffy.

TRADITIONAL GREEN BEAN CASSEROLE

This is the go-to vegetable side dish for Sunday dinners at the Ryan house, with either fried chicken or pot roast as the main event. My mom made this dish while I was growing up, and Ruth prepares her own version, too. Chef Cris has added panko bread crumbs for the topping, and the rich flavors of the sauce and the hot, bubbly combination of butter and sour cream makes this much more interesting than a standard green bean casserole.

The Sunday dinner was something I tried to maintain as a tradition during my playing days, although those long road trips made it a challenge. I remember enjoying pot roast and green beans for dinner after getting Dick Allen, of the Chicago White Sox, to fly out to right on a high fastball on a very hot Sunday afternoon. Allen came up to me after I walked off the mound and said, "You got me." But I considered it kind of a draw, because I didn't strike him out.

SERVES 8
PREP TIME: 10 MINUTES
COOKING TIME: 30 MINUTES

---

4 (14½-ounce) cans French-cut green beans, drained

1 (10¾-ounce) can concentrated cream of mushroom soup

1 cup sour cream

1 teaspoon kosher salt

1 teaspoon cracked black pepper

1½ tablespoons unsalted butter, melted

1 cup coarsely crushed buttery round crackers (such as Ritz)

1 cup panko bread crumbs

---

1 Preheat the oven to 350°F.

2 In a medium bowl, combine the green beans, mushroom soup, sour cream, salt, and pepper. Spoon the mixture into a 2-quart casserole dish. Stir the melted butter into the crushed crackers, and then sprinkle over the top of the casserole.

3 Bake until light brown and bubbly, about 30 minutes.

4 While the casserole is baking, toast the panko bread crumbs on a baking sheet in the oven until golden brown, about 10 minutes. Top the casserole with the toasted bread crumbs. Then ring the dinner bell!

SPINACH CASSEROLE

Like the Spinach Supreme at Del Frisco's in Fort Worth, this spinach casserole is a recipe that provides the texture and flavor of classic creamed spinach without being quite as rich. In this recipe, sour cream replaces heavy cream and panko bread crumbs add just the right amount of crunch. Bob's Steak & Chop House, also in Fort Worth and another one of my favorite restaurants, does a more traditional creamed spinach recipe, which is also quite good. I'm willing to try new and classic ways of doing creamed spinach; it is still my favorite side dish to accompany a perfectly cooked medium-rare filet mignon.

SERVES 6
PREP TIME: 15 MINUTES
COOKING TIME: 25 TO 35 MINUTES

---

1 tablespoon vegetable oil
3 pounds fresh spinach, stemmed and chopped
2 garlic cloves, minced
2 cups sour cream

1 teaspoon garlic powder
1 teaspoon onion powder
1 to 2 teaspoons kosher salt
1 teaspoon freshly ground black pepper

½ cup grated Parmesan cheese
½ cup panko bread crumbs
2 tablespoons unsalted butter, melted

---

1 Preheat the oven to 325°F.

2 Heat the oil in a large saucepan over medium-high heat. Add the spinach and garlic and sauté the spinach until soft, 1 or 2 minutes. Drain the spinach in a colander, and run under cold running water until cool.

3 In a large bowl, mix the sour cream, garlic powder, and onion powder until fully combined.

4 Add the spinach, salt, pepper, and cheese and mix thoroughly.

5 Transfer the mixture to a 9- by 13-inch baking dish, cover with foil, and bake until the top is bubbly, 20 to 25 minutes.

6 Increase the oven temperature to 425°F. Combine the bread crumbs with the melted butter and sprinkle over the top of the casserole.

7 Finish baking until the crust turns golden brown, another 5 to 10 minutes.

8

DESSERTS

TIA MARIA MEXICAN FLAN

Ruth loves the smooth, creamy texture of this Mexican flan.

Growing up, I came to expect a sweet end to a great meal. My mom was an excellent cook, and desserts were her specialty. We had freshly made pies or cakes all the time. Chocolate meringue and coconut meringue pies were her signature desserts. To this day, I have never met anyone who could duplicate her recipes—the meringue had heavenly little beads of caramelized sugar. My mom also made a delicious chocolate cake with chocolate icing.

MAKES 1 (9-INCH) FLAN
PREP TIME: 15 MINUTES, PLUS 2 TO 3 HOURS TO CHILL
COOKING TIME: 1½ HOURS

¾ cup sugar
4 large egg yolks
2 tablespoons Tia Maria (or Kahlúa)

1 teaspoon pure vanilla extract
1½ cups whole milk
¾ cup half-and-half

½ cup sweetened condensed milk
Assorted berries or whipped cream, for garnish

---

1 Preheat the oven to 275°F.

2 Heat the sugar in a medium sauté pan over medium heat until the sugar melts into a syrup-like consistency. Immediately pour the caramelized sugar into the bottom of a 9-inch pie pan. Set aside.

3 Whisk together the egg yolks, Tia Maria, and vanilla in a small bowl. Gradually add the whole milk, half-and-half, and condensed milk and mix well.

4 Pour the mixture over the caramelized sugar in the pie pan.

5 Set the pie pan in a shallow baking pan and pour hot water one-quarter of the way up the side of the pie pan—this is for double-steaming and setting the base of the flan.

6 Bake the flan, uncovered, in the water bath until a knife inserted in the center comes out clean, about 90 minutes.

7 Remove the flan from the water bath and let it cool to room temperature. Chill the flan in the fridge for 2 to 3 hours.

8 When ready to serve, dip the pie pan quickly in hot water, then invert the flan onto a serving dish. Cut the flan into wedges and garnish.

LELA RYAN'S PEPPERMINT ICE CREAM

My mom's peppermint ice cream has always been the perfect fresh-tasting dessert to complement the rich, savory flavors of beef cooked over charcoal. I've asked my sister Jean Ryan-Smith to tell you how to make this Ryan family favorite.

SERVES 8
PREP TIME: 15 MINUTES, PLUS AT LEAST 2 HOURS TO FREEZE

---

4 to 5 large eggs, beaten
1 quart half-and-half

1 tablespoon pure vanilla extract
25 peppermint sticks, crushed fine

1 pinch kosher salt
1 to 2 cups whole milk

---

1 Combine the eggs, half-and-half, vanilla, peppermint sticks, and salt in a medium bowl. Pour the mixture into the container of your ice cream maker.

2 Add as much milk as the ice cream maker will hold.

3 Follow the directions on your ice cream maker for freezing the ice cream.

4 Transfer the ice cream to a container and place a sheet of plastic wrap over the surface. Cover the container tightly and freeze the ice cream until it has hardened, at least 2 hours. It will keep for up to 1 month.

5 Remove the ice cream from the freezer 10 minutes prior to serving, and enjoy.

JEAN RYAN-SMITH: "This ice cream is so refreshing, and the perfect cool-down after eating Mexican food or grilled meats on a hot Texas summer's day. It was a tradition to enjoy this ice cream for dessert after every Ryan family barbecue. You can substitute 2 percent milk for whole milk in this recipe, and the ice cream will still turn out just right every time."

PARIS COFFEE SHOP PECAN PIE

My three favorite pies are pecan, chocolate, and coconut meringue, and they all celebrate the Texas baking traditions I first encountered in my mom's kitchen. My favorite pecan pie is served at the Paris Coffee Shop in Fort Worth. The owner, Mike Smith, is a wonderful baker, and he agreed to share his recipe here. The best part of this recipe is that the pecans are actually inside the filling—not just on the top of the pie!

MAKES 1 (9-INCH) PIE
PREP TIME: 15 MINUTES
COOKING TIME: 30 TO 35 MINUTES

3 tablespoons unsalted butter, melted

2 tablespoons pure vanilla extract

½ cup brown sugar, packed

4 large eggs

3¾ cups pecan halves

1 premade 9-inch pie shell

1 Preheat the oven to 375°F.

2 In the bowl of a standing mixer, or using a hand-held mixer and a medium bowl, cream the butter and vanilla until it becomes a paste.

3 Add the brown sugar and beat until fully mixed with the butter and vanilla.

4 Add the eggs one at a time and beat to combine. Continue beating until almost frothy.

5 Stir in the pecans with a wooden spoon.

6 Pour the filling into the pie shell and bake until the top is brown, 30 to 35 minutes.

BREAD PUDDING WITH WHISKEY SAUCE

The combination of fresh croissants baked in a casserole with whiskey, vanilla, and sugar and then topped with a whiskey sauce made with sour cream and brown sugar is a hit every time. Even if you're not in the mood for dessert, this bread pudding is too good to ignore.

SERVES 8 TO 10
PREP TIME: 15 MINUTES, PLUS 2 HOURS TO REST
COOKING TIME: 1 HOUR AND 10 MINUTES

6 to 8 croissants
1 quart heavy cream
¾ cup sweetened condensed milk

⅓ cup pure vanilla extract
¼ cup Tennessee whiskey
6 large eggs

½ cup plus 2 tablespoons granulated sugar
1 recipe Whiskey Sauce (recipe follows)

1 Preheat the oven to 350°F. Grease a large cast-iron skillet or casserole dish.

2 Cut the croissants into 1-inch cubes and place in the skillet or casserole dish.

3 In the bowl of an electric mixer, or using a hand-held mixer and a large bowl, beat the heavy cream, condensed milk, vanilla, whiskey, eggs, and sugar until the eggs are broken up and the mixture is smooth.

4 Pour the mixture over the croissant pieces. Let the bread pudding sit for 2 hours at room temperature.

5 Place a sheet of parchment paper over the bread pudding and cover the skillet or casserole dish with foil.

6 Bake the bread pudding until firm, about 1 hour.

7 Remove the foil and parchment and put the bread pudding back in the oven for 10 minutes for a golden brown crust.

8 Serve the bread pudding with the whiskey sauce.

Whiskey Sauce

Makes about 1½ cups
Prep time: 5 minutes

¾ cup sour cream
⅓ cup Tennessee whiskey
¼ cup dark brown sugar, packed
2 tablespoons pure vanilla extract

In a small bowl, combine all of the ingredients and mix well. Transfer the sauce to a small server or gravy boat.

SOUTHERN PRALINES

My love for pecans inspired me to ask Chef Cris to whip up a surefire recipe for authentic Southern pralines—a sweet and easy-to-make candy that's always been one of my favorite ways to satisfy a sweet tooth. The flavor combination of pecans, brown sugar, and cinnamon can't be beat. Serve these tasty treats as a perfect conclusion to a perfect meal.

MAKES ABOUT 24 PRALINES
PREP TIME: 10 MINUTES, PLUS 30 MINUTES TO COOL

---

2 cups granulated sugar
½ cup light brown sugar, packed
1 teaspoon baking soda

¼ teaspoon kosher salt
½ teaspoon ground cinnamon
½ cup buttermilk

½ cup (¼ pound) unsalted butter
2 cups pecan halves

---

1 In a small, heavy saucepan over medium heat, combine the granulated sugar, brown sugar, baking soda, salt, cinnamon, and buttermilk. Stir until smooth.

2 Stir in the butter until melted.

3 Insert a candy thermometer into the mixture and, without stirring, bring the temperature to 238°F.

4 Remove the pan from the heat and stir, adding the pecans in small batches and beating briskly with a spoon for 1 minute after each addition.

5 Drop spoonfuls of the praline mixture onto a baking sheet lined with wax paper.

6 Cut each praline to 2 inches in diameter—you can use a cookie cutter to make them uniform.

7 Let the pralines sit until hardened and cool, about 20 minutes. Do not serve warm!

TURTLE CHEESECAKE

Millionaires, a homegrown Texas brand of candy, are made with milk, honey, fresh pecans, and caramel, and are covered in milk chocolate. In 1914 the first Millionaires were made by H. T. Pangburn in the kitchen of his family-owned drugstore in Fort Worth. This cheesecake recipe is based on the Turtle candies made by Pangburn that were a favorite of mine, and are a true Texas tradition.

MAKES 1 (9-INCH) CHEESECAKE
PREP TIME: 25 MINUTES, PLUS 1 DAY TO CHILL
COOKING TIME: 50 MINUTES

---

1 cup pecan pieces
2 cups vanilla wafer cookie crumbs
6 tablespoons unsalted butter, melted

1 (14-ounce) bag caramels
⅔ cup evaporated milk
3 (8-ounce) packages cream cheese, at room temperature

½ cup granulated sugar
1½ teaspoons pure vanilla extract
3 large eggs
½ cups semisweet chocolate chips

---

1 Preheat the oven to 350°F. Butter a 9-inch springform pan.

2 Toast the pecans on a baking sheet in the oven for 6 minutes and set aside to cool.

3 Combine the cookie crumbs and melted butter in a small bowl and press the mixture into the bottom of the pan.

4 Place the pan on a baking sheet and bake for 10 minutes. Remove the pan from the oven and set aside to cool.

5 In a double boiler, or in a metal bowl set over a saucepan of boiling water (don't let the bowl touch the water), melt the caramels in the evaporated milk. Stir until smooth and pour the mixture into the cooled crust.

6 Sprinkle the toasted pecans over the top.

7 In the bowl of an electric mixer, or using a hand-held mixer and a medium bowl, combine the cream cheese, sugar, and vanilla and beat until smooth, scraping down the bowl several times.

8 Add the eggs, one at a time, and beat until smooth.

9 Melt the chocolate chips in the double boiler and whip in the cheese mixture. Pour the batter over the caramel layer.

10 Bake until barely set, about 40 minutes.

11 Cover, refrigerate overnight, and serve cold the following day.

RUTH RYAN'S SPECIAL OCCASION CARROT CAKE

Carrot cake is my favorite dessert. This is Ruth's special recipe, and one that has been a Ryan family favorite for a long time. I've enjoyed this carrot cake on many birthday celebrations and it is always a highlight of the meal. Ruth has experimented with a number of cream cheese frostings, and this is the best she's found—as she says, "It works perfectly every time!"

MAKES 1 (9-INCH) CAKE
PREP TIME: 15 MINUTES
COOKING TIME: 45 MINUTES

For the carrot cake:
2 cups granulated sugar
1½ cups vegetable oil
4 large eggs
2 cups all-purpose flour

2 teaspoons ground cinnamon
2 teaspoons baking soda
2 teaspoons baking powder
1 teaspoon kosher salt
3 cups peeled, grated carrots
½ cup chopped pecans

For the cream cheese frosting:
1 (1-pound) box confectioners' sugar
1 (8-ounce) package cream cheese, at room temperature
¼ cup unsalted butter, at room temperature
2 teaspoons pure vanilla extract

1 Preheat the oven to 350°F. Grease three 9-inch round cake pans.

2 In the bowl of a standing mixer, or using a hand-held mixer and a medium bowl, beat the sugar and oil until blended.

3 Add the eggs one at a time; beat after each addition.

4 Sift the dry ingredients into the mixture and continue beating.

5 Add the carrots and pecans and, using a wooden spoon, mix well.

6 Pour the batter into the cake pans. Bake for 45 minutes.

7 Cool well in the pans before frosting.

8 To prepare the frosting, in the bowl of a standing mixer, or using a hand-held mixer and a medium bowl, combine all of the ingredients and beat until the frosting is a smooth consistency for spreading. (The frosting will seem stiff at first, but after thoroughly mixing, it will soften enough to spread evenly over the cake.)

9 Spread the frosting between each layer of the cake, on top, and on the sides. Serve and enjoy!

ABOUT NOLAN RYAN BEEF & THE COOKBOOK

CHARLIE BRADBURY

President and CEO, Nolan Ryan Beef

This book was written by one of the most successful cattle ranchers in Texas. He just happens to be a Hall of Fame pitcher, but I know another side of Nolan Ryan. I first met Nolan in 1981, when I was working for Beefmaster Breeders United, a beef breed association. I was very young, and my task as a field representative was to visit ranches as part of a voluntary classification program—the rancher paid the field reps to come and tell them which cattle they ought to keep and which cattle they ought to cull (remove from the herd because of undesirable traits that hinder profitability).

Once a rancher agreed to have us inspect the herd, though, they were compelled to abide by our decisions. If there was a young heifer or bull presented by the rancher for classification that we didn't think should retain registration papers, then they would have to surrender the papers—regardless of how they felt about it. It was a very serious process.

Beefmaster Breeders United sent me to Nolan's place in Alvin, Texas, just outside of Houston. Nolan had not been in the Beefmaster cattle business for long at this point. He'd been pitching for the Houston Astros for a year or so, and this was when he started really putting together his cattle herd. He bought a ranch in Gonzalez, but he still kept a lot of his young cattle at his place in Alvin. He had about two hundred acres and he kept young bulls and heifers on his property.

Nolan loved the fact that his cattle were only about thirty minutes from where he pitched at the Astrodome—even during the baseball season he could tend to his cows when the Astros had a home stand.

One of the things I remember about that first visit with Nolan was that he did not like everything I told him about his cattle. When you are dealing with people who are just getting into the purebred cattle business after being successful in another occupation—whether professional sports or the oil business—you generally run into a lot of egos, and you have to watch your step and be diplomatic. But Nolan was different. From the get-go he had a matter-of-fact approach. He viewed this as a business rather than as a hobby or as something he was dabbling in to make some quick money.

Nolan was not out to make a quick buck in the cattle business. He was very conservative with his money and very careful and thoughtful in his investment strategy. Of course, I knew he was a major league pitcher when we first met, but you'd never know based on his demeanor that he was the first baseball player to sign a million-dollar contract. I was a young whippersnapper coming to his ranch as an expert who was paid to make some important decisions he didn't necessarily agree with. He could have been upset with me about some of the things I said, but he didn't come across that way at all—he was interested in and valued my opinion, and he treated me with respect. I could tell he really enjoyed the cattle—it was something he cared about, and that's what leads to success in what is a very challenging business.

Nolan first got into the cattle business in a sort of roundabout way. He started visiting ranches in South Texas because he was interested in deer hunting. The ranches he visited just happened to be Beefmaster ranches (see page 162 for Nolan Ryan's Beefmaster Cattle Guide). Homer Herring was the one who got Nolan started, and he tells the story that they went to look at deer but inevitably ended up spending more time driving around looking at the cattle in the pastures. On one of these "deer hunting trips," Homer remembers that Ruth Ryan was asleep in the backseat of the pickup truck while Nolan and Homer were looking at cows. This was probably not what Homer expected when he invited this hotshot athlete down to South Texas to go deer hunting with him. Nolan really enjoyed Mr. Herring, a fine, old gentleman and quite a character, and he genuinely enjoyed learning about the cattle.

As it happens, Lee Roy Jordan and Chuck Howley of the Dallas Cowboys were both involved in the Beefmaster business at the time, and through those two fellow pro athletes Nolan had the chance to meet Frank Gordon, a barber in Kaufman, Texas, who also happened to raise purebred cattle. Nolan and Frank really hit it off: Nolan would drive around Kaufman to look at Frank's cattle. Eventually he bought a bull from him, and that got him into seriously investing in cattle. As he developed relationships with these two leading developers of the Beefmaster breed, Homer Herring and Frank Gordon, Nolan put his own program together.

From that first meeting as a field inspector, I soon started seeing Nolan at cattle auctions and other cattle-industry events. Nolan was now a Beefmaster breeder, and that had us traveling in the same business and social circles. By the time I met with Nolan about starting Nolan Ryan Beef in 1999, he had grown his business by leaps and bounds. He had served on the board of the Texas Beef Council and had been very involved with promoting beef as a commodity for several years. Governor George W. Bush had appointed Nolan to the Texas Parks and Wildlife Commission, and that position exposed Nolan to a broader section of the cattle-ranching industry. He was also an active leader in the Texas and Southwestern Cattle Raisers Association, the largest state cattlemen's organization in the United States.

By 1999, Nolan had been a member of Beefmaster Breeders United and had served on its board and as its vice president (he later became president of that organization). I had grown my business during this twenty-year period from our first meeting and had become a marketer selling cattle. My wife and I owned a business where we put on auctions and sold cattle all over the country, and most of these auctions involved Beefmaster cattle. I served on the Long-Range Planning Committee for Beefmaster, and Nolan's executive board asked us to take a look at our industry to figure out ways to become more profitable and more efficient.

What we discovered was that the Certified Angus Beef program was so successful that it was impacting the bull-buying decisions of cattle ranchers in traditional markets for Beefmaster cattle. In order for cattle to be eligible for the program, they have to be 51 percent black-hided, with no visible signs of *Bos indicus* genetics and no visible signs of dairy influence. In other words, these cattle didn't have to be pure Angus—they just had to be black-hided. The Angus folks convinced the USDA that the only way you could get black-hided cattle was using Angus, which is (in my opinion) questionable logic at best. At the time, though, they were the only show in town and the first USDA-certified beef program, so they were given a lot of latitude in setting up their specification.

The upshot is that ranchers became convinced that the only way they would get a premium price for their calves is if they were black. Beefmasters were not black, and they exhibited visible signs of *Bos indicus* genetics because they are adapted to southern latitudes, and that was a marketing problem for our organization. The only way we were going to be able to fight this was to come up with our own branded beef program using Beefmaster and other breeds of cattle adapted to the hotter climates of the southern United States, while trying to build a direct bridge to the consumer with a quality product.

Our first step was to dig very deeply into the science of producing great-tasting beef. We worked with some of the best and brightest minds in the academic world of beef to develop unique technology that allows us to ensure that our brand only goes on beef that will produce a tender and flavorful eating experience every time.

We went to the USDA and told them that we wanted to set up a certified program that was based on certifying only tender beef. We first had to convince them that we had the science behind our process. Then we had to come up with a name for the brand. After some initial consumer research, we became convinced that the best branding option was to call our product Beefmaster Beef.

The plan was to produce Beefmaster Beef based on a methodology similar to the Certified Angus Beef model. The USDA told us that in the twenty years since Certified Angus Beef had started, though, things had changed: the USDA had written a regulation that if you wanted to call a brand of beef by a breed name, you then had to prove that each and every animal in your program was at least 50 percent of that breeding. That's a huge undertaking when you can't make the point for purity based on color. It is easy to prove that at least 50 percent of your breed is black if that's the only color, but for a breed without a standard color—Beefmaster cattle can be red, paint, dun, and many other colors— it's much more complicated. We realized it was not feasible to use Beefmaster as our registered brand name.

We had to go back to the drawing board—probably the best thing that ever happened, because that was when we decided to put Nolan's name on the brand. We went to a grocery store in Alvin, Texas, and bought packages of Earl Campbell sausage, Jimmy Dean pork sausage, and Phyllis George's "Chicken by George." We put them in a cooler and drove to the Express Bank, the bank Nolan owned at the time. We all crowded into his small office and stacked these products on his desk. Nolan looked at us as if we were crazy! We told him we wanted him to lend his name to the brand, and in typical Nolan fashion he was very reserved and told us he would think it over.

When he eventually made the decision to move forward, he said something profound that has marked our course ever since. He said that his name on the product would probably convince consumers to try it one time; however, if we did not do our job and manage the process correctly to ensure that the quality was there, they would not be back a second time.

Once he decided to get behind the creation of Nolan Ryan Beef, Nolan's excellent reputation virtually guaranteed the success of the company and its branding operations. We had done some research and found that 73 percent of American households knew who Nolan Ryan was and that he had among the highest approval ratings of any athlete in the history of the survey.

———

Nolan Ryan Beef uses the most wholesome ingredients from cattle raised in a stress-free environment. Our beef cattle are not born and raised in a crate, as movies like *Fast Food Nation* would lead you to believe, and they are certainly not raised on "factory farms."

These cattle are born on grass on ranches, they are raised by their mother, and they have six to eight months until they are weaned and moved to more grass. Typically, after weaning, the calf is then sold to another rancher, often called a stocker or backgrounder, who specializes in raising yearlings. The stocker turns the calves back out on pastures to feed on more grass. They arrive at their new ranch at around 500 pounds and then grow to about 850 pounds by the time they are eighteen to twenty months old.

That is a slow process—1½ to 2 pounds per day, depending on climate. Some calves are raised on wheat until the crop has to be harvested in the spring, while other calves might be raised on native pasture (long-lush grass) in the Flint Hills of Kansas and Nebraska. Cattle have the unique ability to convert low-quality roughage into high-quality protein while grazing rangeland that could never be farmed. Nolan raises many of the cattle that go into our program on his ranches in South Texas and the Texas Hill Country. His cattle typically are grazing native pastures and improved Bermuda grasses.

When the cattle reach a desired target weight of approximately 850 pounds, they are moved to a feedlot where they are fed a grain-based diet for 140 to 160 days prior to harvest. A feedlot is a pretty nice place for a cow to live. Cattle are herd animals by nature; they never like to be alone. In a feedlot they have plenty of room to move around in groups, with a hillside to roam on, fresh water, shade, all the high-quality food they want to eat, and plenty of their buddies to keep them company.

The science says that happy cattle produce great product; it turns out that stress is the single biggest cause of tough steaks. Nolan and other cattle owners treat the animals under their control in a humane way that ensures a safe, pure, and healthy product. Their motivation to do that is the simple truth that contented cattle are more profitable.

———

The goal for Nolan and our company is to produce quality beef for wonderful meals. That's why we worked with Cristobal Vazquez, executive chef at Rangers Ballpark in Arlington and Nolan's personal chef, to produce a practical and inspiring cookbook that will allow you to prepare beef in so many creative ways, based on the southwestern dishes that Nolan enjoyed growing up in Texas. Today, we sell fresh and frozen beef to restaurants and retail customers, and the business is growing rapidly. For more information, visit nolanryanbeef.com.

APPENDIX: NOLAN RYAN'S BEEFMASTER CATTLE GUIDE

In 1931 Tom Lasater began developing Beefmaster cattle, named for their talent for thriving in the arid brush country of South Texas.

Lasater used Hereford, Brahman, and Shorthorns to complement each other to produce Beefmaster cattle.

In 1954 the United States Department of Agriculture (USDA) recognized Beefmasters as a pure beef breed, and as the only certified breed to use a three-way cross. These unique animals, producing the leanest and most tender beef, are bred for the six essentials of Beefmasters selection process:

1 Fertility
2 Disposition
3 Weight
4 Conformation
5 Hardiness
6 Milk Production

What Is a Beefmaster?

½ **Brahman:** Brahmans are known for longevity, hardiness, growth, muscle, and their ability to perform well under the high temperatures of the Texas pastures. They also reproduce up to 50 percent longer than many other breeds.

¼ **Hereford:** Known for adaptability, growth, and fertility, Herefords have been used successfully in beef production since the 1700s.

¼ **Shorthorn:** These heavy milkers (yielding faster-growing calves) are compatible with all other breeds and adapt easily to new environments.

ACKNOWLEDGMENTS

We are very grateful to Michael Sand and everyone at Little, Brown and Company who worked so hard on *The Nolan Ryan Beef & Barbecue Cookbook*, and to Chef Cristobal Vazquez for bringing this book to life with his inspired work on the recipes. A special thanks to David Vigliano, David Peak, and Matt Carlini at Vigliano Associates.

The authors offer heartfelt thanks to Charlie Bradbury, the folks at Nolan Ryan Beef, and the entire Ryan family, especially Ruth, Reid, Reese, Wendy, and Jean Ryan-Smith, for their invaluable help and support. Sincere thanks to Mike Smith at the Paris Coffee Shop in Fort Worth, Texas, for sharing his classic pecan pie recipe. And, finally, thanks to the creative team of photographers Geno Loro and Kelly Gavin, designer Amber Brown, and food stylist Angela Yeung; and to our support staff of Sherry Clawson, Courtney Krug, and Amy Beam.

INDEX

Page numbers in *italics* refer to photographs.

ABOUT THE AUTHORS

Nolan Ryan grew up in Alvin, Texas, and lives in Georgetown. He has had a passion for cattle ranching since childhood. Nolan has served on the board of the Texas Beef Council and on the Texas Parks and Wildlife Commission, and is one of the most influential figures in the beef industry in the United States. Along with his ranching activity he is currently spokesperson for Nolan Ryan Natural Beef.

Nolan distinguished himself as a strikeout leader in his unprecedented twenty-seven seasons in Major League Baseball, playing with the New York Mets (1966; 1968–1971), California Angels (1972–1979), Houston Astros (1980–1988), and Texas Rangers (1989–1993). The all-time leader in strikeouts (5,714) and no-hitters (7), Nolan has owned or shared fifty-three major league records. He also served as chief executive officer of the Texas Rangers, just the third Hall of Fame player to have served as the head of a Major League Baseball franchise.

JR Rosenthal began his writing career as the first California correspondent for *Wine Spectator* in San Francisco and restaurant editor of the *San Jose Mercury News.* He has written six books on baseball, including collaborations with Nolan Ryan, Tony Gwynn, Randy Johnson, and Don Mattingly. With Todd Blackledge of ESPN he is coauthor of *Taste of the Town: A Guided Tour of College Football's Best Places to Eat.*

Cristobal G. Vazquez began his career working for ClubCorp International, the largest owner of private country clubs in the world, as both a *chef de cuisine* and expert ice carver. In addition he headed the culinary team at DNC Sportservice for the past six years as executive chef at the Texas Rangers Ballpark in Arlington.

Charlie Bradbury is president and chief executive officer of Nolan Ryan Beef and is a member of the National Cattlemen's Beef Association. Bradbury received a bachelor of science degree in animal science from Texas A&M University. He lives in Huntsville, Texas, with his wife, Debbie, and three children and owns a small registered cattle ranch.